DANIEL
O'DONNELL

with Eddie Rowley

Living the
Dream

Eddie Rowley is the showbusiness editor of the *Sunday World* and has co-written several bestselling books, including the life stories of Ronan Keating, Mary Byrne, Joe Dolan and Marie Duffy, choreographer of *Lord of the Dance*. He also wrote several books on the life and amazing times of Irish boybands Boyzone and Westlife when they were creating fanmania around the world.

DEDICATION

To my late mother Julia

ACKNOWLEDGEMENT

My heartfelt thanks to everybody who has supported me through the decades in my singing and personal life.

Contents

FOREWORD

FATHER BRIAN D'ARCY

Well over 30 years ago, a young Daniel O'Donnell called to see me in Mount Argus Church in Dublin, where I was then ministering. It was always a pleasure to meet Daniel then, and it has remained so ever since. I was wondering if his new-found fame was difficult to cope with. His reply was precise and memorable: 'I've discovered that the time I'm most myself and most at ease is when I'm on stage.'

Since then I've had the pleasure of seeing Daniel in small intimate gigs, like The Irish Club in Dublin in the early days, and topping the bill in Carnegie Hall, or Branson, Missouri, or The Point in Dublin. This consummate professional performer still is totally himself on stage, singing and entertaining his loyal fans. It's like a vocation. He was born to lift the spirits of his fans, who are, in fact, his friends too.

I am in the privileged position of knowing Daniel from his earliest days – even before he joined his sister Margo's band. The essentially shy young man became confident and competent as soon as he stood before an audience. It's a rare and precious gift and it is the difference between a star and a performer. The latter gets the job done well; real stars, though, willingly give every ounce of themselves to take the audience with them on a memorable experience.

That's what Daniel is – a real star!

I remember watching a young Daniel when he was still at school. He loved dancing to his favourite bands. Even then he stood out. He was dressed to perfection, friendly, mannerly; he was the kind of punter you'd notice for all the right reasons.

With Daniel, what you see is what you get. He's an entertainer who can't believe his luck that myriads of fans are willing to pay good money to see him do what he'd be glad to do for free.

Daniel had his hard days in the beginning. His family was no different from most others in that there were good times and bad times and you learned to grow through both.

Yet once he got a management and a band around him, he not only catapulted to success but revived what was a dying industry in Ireland. His greatest asset was word of mouth. Radio, particularly national radio, was less then helpful in the beginning. Television was largely derisory until the audiences took to Daniel and he became box office. He pulled himself up by the bootstrings. He was counter-culture, but most of all he was himself – natural, happy, clean-cut and singing the music he loved.

I remember sitting in the editor's office in the *Sunday World* buildings in

Dublin 6. We talked about the paper and what could be done to improve it. I suggested we should get in on the Daniel O'Donnell phenomenon right at the beginning. The editorial team weren't aware of Daniel, but they accepted that I was close to the music scene. So they told me to do a short article on the young man making such an impression on the dancing circuit.

I spoke to his manager, Sean Reilly, and then to Daniel himself. The paper sent a photographer, which was unusual. The result was a double-page spread in the *Sunday World*. That proved so popular that, in time, the paper asked Daniel to become a columnist. More than thirty years later, his is still the first page thousands of the readers turn to. He uses his column not to publicise himself but to promote young talented artists looking for a lucky break. Daniel doesn't forget.

In Ireland we have known for decades that Daniel O'Donnell is our most successful entertainer. There were no dips in his career.

With skilful management he was able to move out of dance venues into theatres. He worked hard at his programme and at his ability to keep an audience in the palm of his hand. He gave incredible value for money on stage and then spent hours listening to, encouraging and getting to know every last punter. It was hard work for him and his team, and it couldn't be done for almost four decades unless the star himself was sincere. An artist's integrity comes at a price: a price Daniel is still more than willing to pay.

These days it's common for major visiting artists to spend time with the audience after the show. It wasn't so when Daniel launched his career. He invented the skill of turning fans into loyal friends. His amazing memory for people and faces is a major help. As I said, Daniel doesn't forget.

But it was on the world stage that Daniel's greatest achievements came about.

First it was Britain. Initially he was marketed as a country artist. Then one week there were nine Daniel O'Donnell albums in the Top Ten of the country charts in Britain. It didn't go down well, so they banned Daniel's albums from the country charts (temporarily, as it turned out).

It was a blessing in disguise. He became an entertainer on a wider scale who sold out the biggest venues all over Britain months in advance. The young man from Kincasslagh in Donegal put more bums on seats than any other entertainer. Word of mouth is a powerful medium.

Daniel is a perfectionist when it comes to staging a show. He and Mary Duff led a powerful team of musicians who entertained the masses in the United States, Britain, Australia and New Zealand. The highest professional standards are demanded. Arrangements, musicianship, staging, the programme – all are of the highest quality. It is no accident that he has remained a world star for three decades. That doesn't happen by chance.

Stardom can and does take its toll. Every choice in life rules out some other choice. Nobody can have it all. For Daniel, family and close friends were everything. His late and lovely mother Julia was precious to Daniel. She supported him when times were tough, as they were when his father died so tragically young. She was immensely proud of all her children and she journeyed with Daniel on his climb to the top. She prayed ceaselessly for his success and his safety, and I'm certain she still prays for him from heaven.

She, more than most, understood the loneliness of the long-distance traveller and, like us all, was thrilled when Daniel met Majella, the love of his life. I've presided at many weddings in my priestly life. I look forward to helping couples in love when they decide to commit their lives and their love to each other for ever. It was a privilege to be with Daniel and Majella on their wedding day, which was special in so many ways.

It was covered by all the major channels yet it was intimate and spiritual too. When Daniel left the altar – and left his new bride sitting in the sanctuary – we all wondered what was up. It was only when he started to serenade his Majella from the choir gallery that we recognised it was his special gift to the bride. His speech at the reception was also the best and most sincere tribute I have ever heard from a new groom. Different class.

Since their marriage, it has been beautiful to see how Daniel and Majella have matured together. Love is a gift which no one can demand but which is being lived out with obvious joy and gratitude by Daniel, Majella and their family. It's the perfect personal reward for Daniel, which rightly complements his artistic success.

There are so many aspects to Daniel O'Donnell's life that it is not feasible to be comprehensive. This revised life story, beautifully written with his long-time friend Eddie Rowley, reminds us of the professional and personal achievements of one of the most successful entertainers this country has produced.

Yet the Daniel I meet these days is just as sincere, friendly, helpful and charitable as he always was. If fame has changed him, it is only in the sense that it has magnified his innate goodness.

We all know the sacrifices he made to establish structures in Romania that freed deprived children from a life of hell in state-run institutions there. What isn't as well known is his kindness to people in need and most especially to people with special needs. He knows them all by name, he visits them, he brightens up their lives and they adore him. All of this is done largely in private and unknown to anyone other than their families.

When I first met Daniel, he was a youth with stars in his eyes. He had a dream and a plan and a talent. He knew that hard work will always beat talent when talent refuses to work hard. So he worked hard, and his talent took him to the top. That's why he's still LIVING THE DREAM today. But knowing Daniel as I do, I bet you he still has a dream and a plan that will inspire him, and us, for many years to come.

CHAPTER 1

STRICTLY SPEAKING, I WAS PETRIFIED

Standing in the wings on British television's biggest weekend entertainment show, *Strictly Come Dancing*, while waiting to take the floor for the first time, I was absolutely overcome by a wave of fear and trepidation.

'I don't know what it's like to die, but it can't be much worse than this,' I thought, as I struggled to compose myself.

I took deep breaths and prayed that my legs would carry me on to the floor, despite the fact that they had now turned to jelly. I glanced at my professional dancing partner, the lovely Kristina Rihanoff, who gave me a reassuring smile and a nod as if to say, 'Everything is going to be okay. You can do this.'

Then I heard our names called out: 'Daniel O'Donnell and Kristina Rihanoff!' Suddenly I was being propelled into the scary arena of competitive dancing on live TV.

My heart was jumping out of my chest. But it was too late to turn back.

***

Going back, when the email arrived from the BBC's *Strictly* team inviting me to be a contestant, I couldn't believe what I was reading. I was a huge fan of the show and had often fantasised about dancing on it. As the saying goes, 'Be careful what you wish for.' That was certainly true in my case.

The invitation came at the right time in my life, as it was during a period when I had taken a career break from touring. In the previous decades it would have been impossible for me to take up the offer due to my commitments to live shows in Branson, Missouri at that time of the year.

I was relaxing at our home in Tenerife when the email came through, and I was instantly excited. It was my golden opportunity to shine on *Strictly* as a dancer, or so I imagined.

One of the greatest joys in life for me is dancing. I've always loved jiving and waltzing on the social dancing scene in Ireland. I just never realised how far removed it was from the dance moves I would have to master on *Strictly*.

If somebody had asked me before I did *Strictly*, 'Can you dance?', I would have said 'yes' without any hesitation.

Now I know that what I do at a social event is nothing like real dancing. When it was first announced that I was one of the *Strictly* contestants, a friend of mine sent me a text saying 'Pretend you're in the Irish Club.' That's where we went dancing back in the early 1980s and it was a really fun time in my young life. However, I would soon learn that strutting my stuff in the Irish Club in Dublin was no advantage to me whatsoever on *Strictly*.

I do like a challenge, and I felt that *Strictly* was a great challenge at my time of life. After all, I was fifty-four years old! It demands so much of your brain and your body. When I signed up to *Strictly* I was particularly excited about learning new dance routines. I was hoping to stay in the contest for a good while, or until the end, because it was a great opportunity to get one-on-one coaching from a professional dancer who is among the best in the world. It is in the interests of the professional to bring out the best in you, because if you are voted out of the contest they go too. That's what makes *Strictly* so competitive and so exciting. So I knew I was going to be taught by an expert who wanted to win, and you couldn't buy that kind of training by a professional.

My first week on *Strictly* started on a Tuesday in early September 2015 with rehearsals for the grand opening showpiece, where all the contestants performed with the professionals. Until our first get-together in the *Strictly* studio to practise for that event, it all felt like a dream to me.

The moment I walked into the *Strictly* studio and saw the stairs where everybody walks down on to the show and climbs back up after the performance, the reality hit me. I saw the band and the area where the judges sit, and all around me it seemed that there were hundreds of people working on the big production. That made me instantly aware of the fact that I was involved in the biggest show in Britain. Of all the TV shows I'd done in the world, I'd never experienced an operation like this one. It was overwhelming, but so exciting at the same time.

As we were doing the choreographed piece involving the entire group, I didn't have to worry about the focus being solely on me from the get-go. But I still had to work hard to remember my steps. You realise how much you have to learn when you see the professional dancers dancing together. They are stunning to watch, and then the heart palpatations start when you realise that you have to measure up to that standard in just a couple of weeks.

That Tuesday evening I joined the *Strictly* red-carpet event, where the dancers and celebrities met the media. It was the first time I'd been involved in a red-carpet shindig, and it reminded me of the Oscars. The blinding flashes from the cameras of the small army of photographers would almost make you lose your balance. I walked down the carpet with another contestant, Anita Rani, and the pair of us nearly stumbled. It was a great night and so thrilling to be a part of.

The following morning we had our first dress rehearsal in the studio for the show. By now I had the hang of the routine, or at least I was as good as I was going to get at that stage. There's no slacking for anybody, you have to keep up with it. Every now and then one of us would nudge the other and say, 'Why are we putting ourselves through this? What are we doing here?' But at the same time we were all on a high.

All too soon for us it was showtime, the big moment we'd been working our way up to. Standing at the top of the stairs waiting to be announced was so nerve-racking. But the group dancing went well and judging by the reaction of the audience they loved it too. You'd think One Direction had walked into the room from their wild applause.

The previous year's winner, Caroline Flack, did her showpiece and that was a sight to behold. She obviously had lots of ability, but it's amazing how she developed as a dancer on *Strictly*. She looked like a professional.

There was a clever build-up on the show, with the celebrities and their professional dancers being paired off at intervals. Finally, there was just Peter Andre and myself waiting to be teamed up with a partner. And to my delight I got Kristina Rihanoff.

During rehearsals for the group dance I had danced briefly with Kristina. The celebrities were all in a circle at the time, doing a waltz step. Every ten seconds a new dancer would come to us to give us some advice. Kristina, for me, was the one I felt most comfortable with. She was the one who was the most encouraging to me.

The dancers often request the celebrity they want to work with, and Kristina later disclosed that she had wanted me to be her partner. She thought I might be good at ballroom dancing, even though there's more to it than ballroom. As a fan of *Strictly*, I always felt that Kristina did lovely choreography.

Kristina came to *Strictly* with a lot of experience. She had been a finalist in the world of professional ballroom dancing, as well as being an elite instructor and choreographer.

Born and reared in the bleak naval town of Vladivostok, East Russia, Kristina certainly didn't come from a privileged background, but thanks to her father's love of music she was dancing from an early age.

The outstanding dancer was winning competitions from the time she was seven, and from her teenage years on she became a renowned dance teacher and champion.

After completing university, Kristina got her big break when she was invited to the United States to compete professionally with an American dancer. Later she joined the US TV series *Dancing with the Stars* and was so popular with the public that she was invited to London to take part in *Strictly Come Dancing*.

As I said, the moment I was introduced to Kristina as my dancing partner I felt at ease in her company. As time went on I would discover that she is a lovely, kind, good person.

Kristina has many great attributes, but the one I appreciated the most was her patience. When I was told that my first dance was the waltz, it came as a huge relief.

'Sure I can do that with my eyes closed, no bother,' I thought.

How wrong can you be! The waltz I was used to in the dancehalls of Ireland wasn't remotely like the *Strictly* dance that Kristina began to teach me. They weren't from the same family!

When I saw what they call 'the geography of the dance', I realised that I had so much to learn in order to get the steps right and to coordinate all my body movements. There was a lot to master in the movements of the feet. Then there was the positioning of the rest of my body, holding myself properly in the dance and keeping my figure in the right position. You have to move almost like a robot, but it's beautiful when it's done properly because it looks like you are gliding around the floor. I still had a long way to go before I made it look beautiful.

When I got my feet and body into some kind of organisation, I had my head to think about. Your head is supposed to be steady, but mine was like Virgil, the puppet out of an old British TV show called *Thunderbirds* ... wobbling and tilting like it was on a string!

Oh boy, it was a huge amount of work. There were many times when I stopped and thought, 'Why did I want to do this?' But there was no going back. I could see that the road back was further than the one ahead, so it was better to keep going. But I was raging with myself that it was taking so long to master the waltz. I wanted to be able to do it there and then.

Everything goes so fast in the training that it's hard to keep up. When you master the smallest thing there's a great sense of achievement, but you don't have time to shout 'yeesss!' because you'll have missed the next bit.

The depth of petite Kristina's patience was bottomless, even as time went on. She has a wonderful ability to teach and a fantastic way of teaching. I really don't know how any of the professionals have the patience to train up contestants from scratch in such a short time for a major TV show. I'd look at Kristina demonstrating a move and it would be so graceful and effortless. Then I'd try it and I would be just plain awkward.

It was so daunting, but Kristina never let it overpower me. If there was something beating me, she would strip it back and make it simpler until I could understand it. And then she'd build it up to where it needed to be. I would constantly hear her say, 'That was good!', even though it probably wasn't good at all. But she was working on my confidence as well as my dancing. And I would discover that so much of how you perform is to do with confidence.

Kristina remained very calm all through the process. At no point did she ever say, 'That was wrong!' Instead, she would pick me up and say, 'Just try and do it this way.' She never seemed to get frustrated with me, and I would say I put her as far out to the limit as she's ever been. Her early background as a dance teacher really shone through.

I think the problem with me, as with a lot of people, is that we slump into our bodies. Although I was as fit as a fiddle, I had to work on what they called my core strength, so I was sent off to a gym twice a week to build that up and straighten my physique. I reckoned I was going to be a couple of inches taller by the end of it. Dancing is incredibly good for your posture.

I was now living in a small rented apartment in London for the duration of my stint on *Strictly*. I love London – it's a great city with so many attractions, including all those marvellous West End theatre shows – but every night when I returned home after a day of rehearsals I was too tired to do anything.

Before rehearsals began for my competitive dancing I went to see a couple of West End shows with Majella when we were settling in to the apartment. We both loved the Carole King musical, *Beautiful*, which tells the story of the hit songwriter's remarkable rise to stardom with songs like '(You Make Me Feel Like) A Natural Woman', 'You've Got a Friend', 'Up on the Roof' and 'Locomotion'. On the following night we went to see the musical *Kinky Boots*, which features music and lyrics by Cyndi Lauper.

After those nights out, my whole world was consumed with mastering my dance routine. My mind never took a break from it, even when I went to sleep. I'd suddenly open my eyes at three or four in the morning and the dance would be swirling around in my brain. Then I'd turn on the light, shoot out of bed and begin practising my steps over and over.

In the daytime, as I strutted along London streets, I'd often be in my own world of dance. Suddenly my arms would go up and I'd do a few steps. I was totally oblivious to everyone around me in that moment as I waltzed along the city thoroughfare on my way to rehearsals. I'm sure many people who saw me going through those motions must have assumed it was some kind of candid camera scene. I was so engaged with the dance that I didn't care who saw me.

Kristina impressed on me the importance of taking a break from the dance to give my mind a rest, so as I had the following weekend off I went to see one of my friends, country singer John McNicholl, perfoming at St Joseph's Club in Highgate. John and his band were brilliant and I even got up to sing a couple of songs with them. Then I took to the floor to dance in the old style that I was used to. In that moment I realised that social dancing doesn't require much skill at all.

All of the people I met that night promised to vote for me when *Strictly* went live on the telly.

The following morning I woke up feeling exhausted. This had nothing to do with the previous night's dance. It was my body reacting to the stress of the previous week, trying to master my *Strictly* performance.

I was up early the following Monday when my coaching with Kristina began at 9am. We worked right through to 3pm, and at the end of the session I felt for the first time that I had improved immensely. I'd never put so much into anyting I'd done before in my life, and I'd always given 100 per cent in my career.

That night I went to a ball in the Mansion House, London, for the Dot Com Children's Foundation, as Kristina is a Trustee of the charity. I was so impressed hearing Kristina speak about the charity and how it helps young children in difficult situations. This is a side to her that the media hadn't focused on. She is such a genuinely decent and generous person. The ball raised £80,000 that night for the charity.

As I had a day off on the Tuesday, I went for a round of golf with friends at the Muswell Hill Golf Club. I was with my brother-in-law, Michael, and a friend called Oliver Foye, who was celebrating his 80th birthday. The club pro joined us and it was an enjoyable afternoon where I cleared my head.

Over the next couple of days my dancing got better and better.

'You should be proud of yourself,' Kristina said, patting me on the back.

'Well, it's you that has got me to where I am,' I told her.

Over lunch with Kristina I realised that she's a lovely person to be around, which was just as well as we spent all day every day together dancing. We would usually go for lunch together in one of the many lovely local cafés. Whenever people recognised us they would stop and wish us good luck.

***

In the world of reality television they call the experience of participating in the show 'the journey'. So I was on a whole new 'journey' in my life, and I wasn't alone. There were fourteen other contestants on 'the journey' with me.

I struck up an early 'bromance' with two them, Iwan Thomas and Peter Andre, when we did some of the show's promotion together. But as time went on I got to know the rest of the team and we became a great bunch of friends.

Strictly was a struggle for all of us, so we each knew what the others were going through. Even though it was a competition, there was tremendous goodwill among the group as we all encouraged and applauded each other. Before long, we had set up our WhatsApp group to share our individual experiences, our jokes, our laughs, our aches and pains and our woes. Jeremy Vine said at one stage that even his ears were sore. I wondered what kind of a dance he was doing!

We had all come from different backgrounds. Iwan, whose professional dance partner was Ola Jordan, is a British Olympic medallist and sports commentator. Best known as a 400m runner, he was a Commonwealth and European champion and remains the British record holder in the 400m.

Professional boxer Anthony Ogogo, described as the Golden Boy of the boxing ring, had been undefeated in his professional career. He won a bronze medal in the 2012 London Olympics and had a postbox in his home town of Lowestoft, Suffolk, painted bronze in his honour. Anthony's partner was Oti Mabuse.

Celebrity chef Ainsley Harriott, of the TV show *Ready Steady Cook*, said his only footwork experience was 'dancing around the kitchen with Suzy Salt and Percy Pepper'. Ainsley, who was partnered by Natalie Lowe, is definitely larger than life. He would dominate the room in a fun way when he arrived.

With her popular afternoon slot on Sky Sports News, Kirsty Gallacher was a well known face on sports television. The daughter of one of Britain's legendary golfers and former Ryder Cup captain Bernard Gallacher, she proved her sporting prowess when she won the third series of Channel 4's winter sports series *The Games*. Kirsty's *Strictly* partner was Brendan Cole.

Carol Kirkwood is one of the BBC's most experienced and beloved weather presenters, best known for presenting the weather on *BBC Breakfast*. She had won Best TV Weather Presenter seven times. Carol was paired with the show's most successful professional dancer, Pasha Kovalev.

BBC broadcaster and journalist Jeremy Vine made his name as the presenter of BBC One's *Points of View* and the quiz show *Eggheads*, as well as *The Jeremy Vine Show* on BBC Radio 2. His partner was Karen Clifton.

R&B singer Jamelia had enjoyed numerous hits, including a song called 'Superstar'. She was also a regular panelist on the *Loose Women* TV show. Jamelia's *Strictly* dance partner was Irishman Tristan MacManus from Bray, County Wicklow.

Actress Helen George from Birmingham was famous for playing the role of Nurse Trixie Franklin, a 1950s midwife in the BBC series *Call the Midwife*, set in London's East End. It was a huge hit, with viewing figures of 11 million on a Sunday evening. Helen's *Strictly* partner was Aljaz Skorjanec.

TV presenter Anita Rani had become a household name for her work on BBC One TV shows *Countryfile*, *Watchdog* and *The One Show*. Anita was partnered by Gleb Savchenko.

As landlady Linda Carter in the legendary Queen Vic in *EastEnders*, Kellie Bright had picked up 'Best Actress' and 'Best Dramatic Performance' at The British Soap Awards that year. Kellie's professional dance partner was Kevin Clifton.

Actress Georgia May Foote had famously played the role of Katy Armstrong in *Coronation Street* between 2010 and 2015. From her on-screen relationship with Chesney Brown, becoming a mother and beginning an affair with Ryan Connor, the twists and turns of Katy's life gripped the nation during Georgia's five-year stretch in the soap. Georgia's dance partner was Giovanni Pernice.

Katie Derham was 'the face' of BBC Proms. She had been presenting the BBC's coverage of the yearly musical extravaganza for the previous six years, as well as working on many other shows on TV and radio. Katie was partnered on *Strictly* by Anton Du Becke.

Pop heart-throb Jay McGuiness had shot to fame in the massively successful boyband The Wanted. The group enjoyed two UK number one singles with 'All Time Low' and 'Glad You Came'. Even though boybands are known for their slick dance moves, Jay pointed out that The Wanted were too cool for that kind of carry on, so he had little or no experience of dancing. Jay's partner was Aliona Vilani, who insisted that the first thing he should do was get rid of his shoulder length locks.

Peter Andre, of course, was also a former pop star who went on to make a career in reality TV. As a singer, Peter became the sixth highest-selling artist in the world with chart-topping pop songs 'Mysterious Girl' and 'Flava'. His next wave of fame came when he took part in the third TV series of *I'm a Celebrity ... Get Me Out of Here!*, which led to him landing a documentary franchise about his life. Peter was partnered on *Strictly* by Janette Manrara.

Peter was an early favourite with the bookies to win *Strictly*. When we first started dancing together as a group, I could see that he was a very impressive performer. He had all the moves and I reckoned he had a good healthy competitive streak as well. The other striking thing that Peter possessed was a six-pack. I just had the one-pack, so I was clearly at a disadvantage in that department!

However, like myself, Peter was fighting the jitters ahead of dancing live on the show. He said in interviews that he was really anxious about stepping into the ballroom. After turning down offers in the past, Peter had finally said yes to the *Strictly* challenge because it had come at the right time in his life. But he admitted that he hadn't anticipated how nerve-racking it was going to be.

And that's exactly how I was feeling.

CHAPTER 2

FACING THE JUDGES

*S*trictly Come Dancing, of course, is not just about the spectacle involving the professional dancers and their celebrity contestants. The show's panel of judges, who would publicly critique my moves on the dance floor, are also stars of the winning formula that has made it Britain's top family entertainment show.

The judge we all feared, naturally, was Craig Revel Horwood, who is very hard to please. He certainly doesn't pull any punches and is famous for his withering comments. Craig came to *Strictly* with a lot of experience.

Born in a sleepy Australian town called Ballarat, Victoria, when he was old enough Craig moved to the bright lights of Melbourne, where his dance career began as he appeared in shows like *West Side Story* and *Me and My Girl*.

Craig eventually headed to Europe, where he joined the Lido de Paris as a dancer in *Panache*, and then became a principal singer in *Formidable* at the Moulin Rouge. A year later he was in the UK tour of *Cats*, performing in Edinburgh and Dublin. He also performed in *Cats* and *Miss Saigon* in London's West End.

'I'm very lucky I chose to do dance and music as a child because it has brought about the most amazing opportunities in my life,' Craig said one day, adding: 'I've been very lucky to have had the opportunity to perform in loads of musicals in my life, and then the chance to do *Strictly Come Dancing* came along.'

Craig admitted that nobody predicted the worldwide success of *Strictly*. 'We didn't think it would last, but it has taken the world by storm,' he said. 'It has broken the *Guinness Book of World Records* for the most produced format in the world. When we started out in 2004 we thought it was going to be one evening of Saturday night entertainment. It has really changed the face of how people think about dancing, their knowledge of dancing, and it has produced a million spin-off shows, which is fantastic.'

I have to say, I did like Craig, because away from the camera and his role as a judge he's a really nice guy and very funny. On the show, of course, every contestant dreads his comments, but that's what gives the *Strictly* panel a bit of edge.

The most flamboyant judge on the panel is without doubt Bruno Tonioli. He's just hilarious. Bruno is a smallish man with a massive personality and he almost explodes with passion when he's delivering his comments. He knows what he's talking about too, being one of the world's top choreographers and having worked on shows with legends of showbiz, including Elton John, Michael Jackson, Freddie Mercury, Tina Turner and Paul McCartney.

Bruno grew up in Ferrara, a small town in north-east Italy. He knew what he wanted to do in life from a very early age after seeing the musical *Cabaret* when it came out in 1972. Bruno was so excited by *Cabaret* that he went to see it eight times in a row. When he told his parents about his ambition to be a dancer, they weren't impressed. Bruno's mother and father wanted him to get a good, steady, secure job working in a bank. However, like I would do in my own life, young Bruno followed his dream and against their wishes he went to Rome and started ballet lessons.

Bruno left Italy at the age of eighteen to work with the Paris-based dance company La Grande Eugene before moving to London and making it his home. He worked as a freelance dancer in the UK, with one of his notable appearances being in Elton John's video for 'I'm Still Standing', and made the move over to choreography when he went to work on the legendary British TV show *Not The Nine O'Clock News*.

Judge Darcey Bussell has a gorgeous personality and she's so kind to contestants while giving constructive criticism. I remember reading an interview where Darcey said she could tell if someone is a good dancer or not in three seconds flat. She said she can tell by watching how a person walks, as she can see how supple their body is, and whether or not they have tight hips. She also said that everybody can dance: it's only their inhibitions that hold them back.

Darcey is a former principal dancer with The Royal Ballet and one of the most famous British dancers of all time. She was promoted to principal in 1989, at just 20 years old. She retired from the company in 2007 and joined the *Strictly* judging panel in 2009. Darcey came out of retirement briefly to dance the 'Spirit of the Flame', leading a troupe of two hundred dancers at the 2012 London Olympics closing ceremony.

The head judge, Len Goodman, had actually given me a score of 10 points before *Strictly* even began. Just a couple of months earlier, Len was doing a BBC One TV programme called *Holiday of My Lifetime*, where he took well-known people back in time to recreate their childhood holidays. I was asked to do it and I brought him to Owey and Arranmore islands off the coast of Donegal. During the show we attended a céilí – an afternoon of traditional dancing – on Arranmore.

When it was over, Len said to the crowd: 'I was watching Daniel and he has great posture. Don't you think they should have him on *Strictly?*'

Then he produced his lollipop with the number 10 on it, and declared, 'It's a ten from Len!'

Len didn't know that I had already been selected for *Strictly*, and I couldn't tell him because I had been sworn to secrecy. There are only three or four people at the BBC who are involved in the selection, and it's all very James Bond-ish because it's so top secret until the time comes to announce the names. I was terrified of letting it slip, even to Len.

I loved Len on *Strictly* and was sad to see him retire after the 2016 series ended. Len has a very colourful background as he started life as a welder in the London Docks. He was soccer mad at the time and went on to pursue his passion for football before injury ended his career prospects in that game. Next Len then took up ballroom dancing and specialised in a form of dance called Exhibition, which is all about the lifts. He quickly became a British champion, winning the title four times. On *Strictly* Len was more concerned about peformance than technique. He was looking for good interaction between the couples and did not want to see any nerves surfacing on the night.

From the get-go, my nerves were absolutely determined to surface as soon as I got set to step on to the *Strictly* dancefloor.

And I couldn't control them.

***

Two days before my first live performance on Saturday, 25 September, I got my first taste of the *Strictly* ballroom when we did our rehearsals for the show. When I got out on the floor I wasn't able to catch my breath, it was so overwhelming. I had never felt a sensation like it. I couldn't believe how nervous I was.

It was also quite emotional for me as there were scenes of Ireland all around the *Strictly* room, with shamrocks and a river beamed onto the floor through the magic of stage lighting. The song chosen for our waltz was 'When Irish Eyes Are Smiling', sung by Ruby Murray. I thought it was very respectful that the BBC picked an Irish song for the dance.

The late Ruby Murray from Belfast had been one of the most popular singers in the UK and Ireland back in the 1950s. I never knew Ruby or got to see her live, but I loved her voice. She was like one of those iconic singers from the early era of Hollywood. Ruby had been our friend all through rehearsals on a recording, and hers was a very pleasant voice to dance to.

I noticed on the schedule during the week leading up to the show that Friday was spray tan day! I think it was for parts of the body that were going to be exposed. I intended to be more covered than exposed. There are parts of me that nobody needs to see. And I'm not a great one for showing off the chest.

Friday started for me with a trip to the gym, where I was going to be working with a professional trainer. Kristina told me not to do too much, and the trainer advised me that half an hour a day was plenty for core strength.

Then came Saturday night, and here I was in the wings with Kristina waiting for our cue to dance. I was in bits, but before I knew it I was whirling around the floor with Kristina in my arms and then I went into some kind of a daze. There was a period during that dance on live television where I didn't know who I was, I didn't know who Kristina was. There was a moment where I thought, 'Who are you? What are you doing here?' That probably happened in a second, but it felt like an hour.

When the dance ended and we went to the judges for their comments I couldn't speak, I was so nervous. I thought I had made a huge blunder on the floor. It was only later when I looked at a recording of the performance that I realised everything had looked fine. I had forgotten a wee bit of the routine, but we did other things that weren't planned – that's where a professional dancer can plaster over the cracks – and the dance looked okay. However, I was in such a daze afterwards that the judges' comments didn't register with me in the immediate aftermath.

Judge Craig Revel-Horwood had harsh words, describing my performance as 'pretty uneventful'. Naturally I was very disappointed by Craig's comments, but he was outnumbered by the rest of the judging panel.

Len Goodman said my hold 'could have been stronger', but he added that I had the best footwork he'd ever seen. Good old Len; I was delighted with that observation. When she was coaching me, Kristina had said to me that you need to pretend you are drawing a picture and painting your dance on the floor with your feet. It was certainly what Len noticed.

'It was very collected, very well placed and very, very pleasing,' judge

Bruno Tonioli said. Bruno gave me a real lift and a confidence boost as well with those words.

Darcey Bussell was also very kind to me in her comments, saying: 'You danced like the perfect gentleman. I know there are nerves out there but just relax your back and look at Kristina as much as you can.'

My total score from the judges for my first dance was 24 out of 40. That got me through to the next round, as there was no public vote on the first show. It was the following Tuesday before I recovered from the ordeal. Kristina, once again, was very encouraging and determined to get me back on track.

'You forgot a bit of the routine, but you did well,' she said.

However, as we talked Kristina admitted that for a moment she thought there was something wrong with me on the dancefloor during the performance, as she saw my eyes glaze over.

When I explained what had happened, she said: 'This happens with nerves and you must learn from that. You must learn to stay in the moment, be in control, think about your dancing and think about what you are doing.'

And when I reflected, I realised I wasn't totally focusing on my dance that night. I think that's what happened to me. And when I was in front of the judges I was thinking about the mess I had made when I shouldn't have given it a thought, because it wasn't a mess at all.

Now I had a clean slate and I was back in rehearsals, learning a new dance routine. This time it was the Charleston, which was the dance I didn't want because it's a tough one. To make matters worse, I had picked up a cold. I remember telling Donegal's Highland Radio in an interview that week how I was determined that the show would go on, despite my cold.

Then I added: 'As long as it doesn't go into the feet. If I get foot and mouth I'm finished.' If I didn't keep my sense of humour I certainly would have been finished.

Seriously though, I always want to be the best at whatever I do, or at least do whatever I'm doing to the best of my ability. I will certainly put in the work and the dedication and after that there's not a lot more you can do. But God help poor Kristina, she was going to have another hard week ahead of her teaching me the Charleston.

I had got a break away from it all on the Monday night when we attended the Pride of Britain Awards in the Grosvenor Hotel on London's Park Lane. The awards honour British people who have acted bravely or extraordinarily in challenging situations. It was a great night of celebrity spotting – I'm just a fan like everyone else – and we got to meet famous people like Sharon and Ozzy Osbourne; Michael Flatley and his wife, Niamh; Eamonn Holmes and his wife, Ruth Langsford; Phillip Schofield; Holly Willoughby; Carol Vorderman; and even the great soccer legend David Beckham, who I shook hands with. It was a fantastic night.

The rest of the week was all about the Charleston, a dance that became popular in the 1920s. Danced by both young women and young men of that generation, the Charleston involved fast-paced swinging of the legs as well as big arm movements. Because young women kicked their legs up with abandon while doing the Charleston, it was considered one of the most scandalous dances of its time.

When I was learning it I felt like my arms were on hinges and elastic bands – they were flying everywhere. As I glanced in the mirror during rehearsals I realised I looked ridiculous. But I had to get it right because the first elimination was going to happen on the Sunday night of that weekend. I certainly didn't want to be the first to go, but I didn't want anybody else to go either because we all got on so well and were now friends. Before going on to *Strictly* I didn't know any of the other contestants, but now we were having such a good time together. We were all happy together and frightened together and terrified together. It was a host of emotions.

On Tuesday of that week we took a trip to Royal Windsor Racecourse to record a scene for *Strictly* as my dance had a horse-racing theme. Afterwards there was time for a little relaxation, so Majella, Kristina and myself enjoyed some afternoon tea at the famous racecourse.

Back in the dance studio on Wednesday I was still struggling with the Charleston. 'It's not easy when you're fifty-three and you're carrying thirteen stone around the floor,' I told Kristina. She kept reminding me to stay in the moment and to think about my dancing. The Charleston is really fast, and I was meeting myself coming back. Once again I heard myself asking the question, 'Why did I say "yes" to this?!'

But the show must go on.

Coming up to show night I saw one headline that read: 'Irish stallion Daniel O'Donnell tackles the Charleston on *Strictly Come Dancing*.'

That made me laugh out loud. When I looked in the mirror all I could see was a Connemara pony.

On the night of the performance my nerves were back, but I kept on smiling and put them back in their box as Kristina and I romped through our routine to the song, 'Let's Misbehave'. The dance went well, and I even managed to do a lift without dropping poor old Kristina. I'm not sure which of us was more relieved.

Afterwards, Bruno said that I waned towards the end of the ninety-second dance, adding: 'You need to go full gallop all the time. You gotta keep going.'

I reminded him: 'This is a fifty-three-year-old horse you're talking about.'

Then I held my breath as Craig gave his judgement – and I nearly fainted when I heard him say: 'You have fantastic rhythm and there is a dancer lurking within.'

Even if I can't find him, the fact that he's lurking is good enough for me, I thought.

Darcey was equally complimentary, telling me that I 'came alive', and adding: 'For me, you had great energy throughout. Honestly, I was not expecting that!'

Len predicted that we would make it through to the next round, but of course we had to wait for the public vote to come in.

Standing at the top of the stairs before the *Strictly* results come through is the worst feeling in the world. It's very traumatic waiting to know your fate. Even if it's not you that's leaving it's going to be one of your friends, and that's just as difficult.

As luck would have it, Kristina and myself were the first to be put through to the following weekend. It was a huge relief. In a moment of euphoria I screamed and lifted Kristina off her feet.

Then came a crushing blow when Iwan was the first celebrity to be voted out of the show. As I said, Iwan, Peter and myself were the three amigos. Afterwards, Iwan remarked that going up against the *Strictly* judges was 'more nerve-racking than the Olympics'.

***

When you're on a show like *Strictly*, you're in a bubble. It's as if the outside world doesn't exist, or at least that's how it seemed to me. You forget that millions of people are watching you on live television every weekend. And

I never thought about the impact or the attention it was receiving back home in Donegal.

It was my niece, Patricia, who told me about the support I was getting in my native county. There were banners displayed all around Donegal wishing me luck. I heard that some locals had even made trips to the North of Ireland canvassing people to vote for me. I didn't anticipate that level of interest, but I was absolutely delighted that everybody at home was entering into the fun of it.

***

After the high of surviving the Charleston, I was back to earth with a bang the following week when it was revealed that our next dance was the cha-cha-cha, also simply known as the cha-cha and of Cuban origin.

Going into the competition I was worried about having to do a Latin dance, so now I had to literally step up and take it on. Kristina and myself would be perfoming it in character as Sandy and Danny from *Grease* and dancing to the big *Grease* number, 'Summer Nights'.

The cha-cha rehearsals didn't start off well that week. I couldn't get the moves into my head, never mind my feet. When I get nervous my legs go weak, and that made it worse. I kept thinking about having to do this dance on live TV and looking like a fool, and I wanted to run away. Too late for that, of course, so I just had to knuckle down and work hard. Kristina kept telling me not to be too hard on myself. But after a day in the studio with Kristina I'd go back to my apartment and practise, practise, practise.

On the Thursday before the show, Kristina decided that I needed to take a break and clear my mind. So that night she took me to the International

Ballroom Dancing Championships at the Royal Albert Hall. I loved watching everybody dancing in their beautiful costumes. The audience was invited up to dance, and Kristina and myself took to the floor. People recognised us from *Strictly* and were wishing us success on the show. There is so much affection for *Strictly* and the contestants and I realised that I picked the right reality TV show to have a go. Wild horses wouldn't drag me on to shows like *I'm a Celebrity ... Get Me Out of Here!* or *Celebrity Big Brother.*

On the night of our cha-cha-cha dance I summoned up my inner Danny Zuko, flicked up my quiff, and off I went with Kristina. The nerves were no better, but I got through the routine without making a hash of it. Kristina gave me a reassuring hug as we faced the judges. The reviews were mixed, but honest.

Darcey said: 'It was a bit soft. I would have loved it to have been a bit crisper and cleaner.'

Len remarked: 'It was a mix between "Summer Nights" and "Last Of The Summer Wine".'

Bruno told me that I was 'skipping along all the time, something you don't do in the cha-cha-cha'.

Craig was actually very complimentary, noting that I did remember the choreography and my timing was 'very good'.

However, we received the lowest judges' score, with 21 out of 40.

Kristina said afterwards that I inspired huge pride in her as a teacher, adding that ballroom routines suited me better than Latin. She said on Twitter that I was a non-dancer trying my best and I did so good.

There was good news when the public votes were announced on the following night's show. The public decided that I should go through to the next round to dance the foxtrot with Kristina.

Sadly, it was Olympic medal-winning boxer Anthony Ogogo and his partner Oti Mabuse who were sent home, after losing out in a dance-off with Ainsley Harriott and Natalie Lowe.

So I lived to fight another day, but the following week I didn't get a burst of confidence about my chances of staying in the contest for much longer as I set about mastering the the American smooth foxtrot for our next outing on the *Strictly* dance floor. It was a big challenge, as we had only twenty hours each week to learn a new dance.

I always thought I could dance the foxtrot, but the American smooth is a different animal altogether. It even has lifts, so I was hoping that *Strictly* had plenty of insurance cover.

Majella was in London with me and during that week we both attended a fabulous event at the Royal Albert Hall where our friend Cliff Richard celebrated his seventy-fifth birthday during his concert. There were lots of Cliff's pals in the audience, including *Grease* icon Olivia Newton-John, Brian May of the rock group Queen, and Michael Flatley from *Lord of the Dance*.

Our night with Cliff was a highlight of the week, and it was lovely to see him on top form after all the dark days he had endured in recent times. Back in our rehearsal studio I found Kristina very upset that week. A newspaper headline had quoted her as saying that she believed we wouldn't win *Strictly* because I'm an old man. I could see that Kristina was genuinely hurt by the story and she denied it completely.

'For goodness sake, Kristina, don't be annoying yourself about it, sure you know to look at me that I'm not old,' I joked, trying to cheer her up.

I reassured Kristina that, firstly, the story didn't bother me in the slightest, and, secondly, I totally accepted that she never made the comment.

It wasn't age that was going to prevent me from winning *Strictly*. I felt the nerves were going to do me in unless I got a handle on them. They were still gripping me the moment I heard my name called out to dance. It was even an effort to just walk down the steps.

Standing by Kristina's side on the Saturday night, dressed in my airline captain's uniform and cap as we got set to dance the American smooth to Frank Sinatra's 'Fly Me to the Moon', I was less nervous than on the previous shows. I kept telling myself, 'I can do it! I can do it!'

Out on the floor, I felt I had a good take-off and a smooth landing, and I managed the lifts without dropping Kristina. That was a good result in my book. But, of course, the judges had their own take on my performance.

Bruno said my dancing was 'premium economy' and told me to have more confidence.

I joked: 'We might have hit an air pocket or two.'

Craig wasn't full of praise, but he was encouraging, saying: 'That number needs swing and sway and I think you got it right but it was lacking in style. Daniel, you have musicality on your side but it needs to be more dynamic.'

Darcey noted that my lifts were 'seamless and very good', adding: 'Throw those nerves away and give more and more.'

Len remarked: 'You must have been on EasyJet because there was a lovely flow to it – there's a charm and an elegance to it. But you need to go for it little bit more.'

We scored 23, two points more than the previous week.

However, when the results of the public vote came through, Kristina and myself were in the bottom two with Kirsty and Brendan, who had danced to U2's 'Beautiful Day'.

That, of course, meant we were now facing into a dance-off.

My second attempt at the American smooth did not go well, as I made some early mistakes which threw me for the rest of the dance. Maybe my subconscious realised the exit door was open, and was afraid it was going to close before I got to it. But I didn't deliberately forget anything. I just genuinely went wrong and when you go wrong it's very hard to pick up.

At the end of the dance-off, Craig said: 'One couple did really, really well in the dance-off and one couple I'm afraid made a lot of mistakes. I am going for the couple that was the most powerful, and that was Kirsty and Brendan.'

Darcey agreed. 'The couple I would like to save is Kirsty and Brendan,' she said.

It was the same result from Bruno, who said: 'I would like to keep the couple that actually committed less mistakes tonight, and that is Kirsty and Brendan.'

It was all over for Kristina and myself at that point. When host Tess Daly asked Len for his opinion, he said: 'I did agree.' He had gone for Kirsty and Brendan too.

Kristina was quite emotional, but to be honest I was relieved to be going home at that point.

'Fly Me to the Moon': I was over the moon!

Looking back, I have no regrets about taking on the *Strictly* challenge when I was fifty-three years of age and nearly thirty-five years in show-business. I would hate to be sitting here today wondering what it would have been like. At least now I know that it wasn't for me, but at least I won't die wondering. This time I definitely bit off more than I could chew, but I had to do it to realise that.

In truth, that has been the journey of my life. I've taken on challenges every step of the way and it has given me a career and a life beyond all my dreams and great expectations.

And that life began on 12 December 1961, in one of the most beautiful parts of the world ... my beloved Tír Chonaill (Donegal).

CHAPTER 3

KINCASSLAGH

Although I was never conscious of it as a wee lad, I grew up in poor circumstances. But I obviously had a happy childhood, because looking back I have fond memories of that era. The house that was our home during my early years was very basic. It was an old-fashioned two-storey residence with an open-hearth fire that had pots hanging from crooks and simmering over hot coals. Even the scones (as we called the bread and cakes) were baked in a pot 'oven' on the open fire. My grandmother used to say that she carried stones for the building of the house, which was erected in the late 1800s. We didn't own it. It belonged to my mother's cousin, and it is still there today, situated across from the council house that later became our home.

Our living conditions were fairly primitive. There was no water supply laid on and we had to draw water from our neighbour Annie's well across the road; we didn't have a bathroom and the toilet was a tin hut across the road. I can recall only one family who had a flush toilet and I used to be mesmerised by it.

Nowadays, children are bathed on a regular basis, sometimes daily. But in those days there was a big 'scrub up' in a tub in front of the open fire in the kitchen-cum-livingroom on a Saturday night. And that was it. I don't remember getting washed during the week. It wasn't that I was a dirty wee bugger or anything, but I don't remember being washed every night. There wasn't so much emphasis on that in those days. We must have been rotten at school during the week! I often think now, how did the teachers put up with us then?

In 1967, a year before my father died, we got a new house from Donegal County Council. At the time, it was like moving into a space ship. It had a bathroom. And a toilet. And taps. God, the fun I had turning on and off those taps, watching the water gushing out of the little pipes. Magic. Boy, we were really coming up in the world! It was wonderful moving into that grand house.

The world beyond in those days wasn't very important. To me, nothing existed outside our little close-knit community. Kincasslagh, a small fishing village on the north-west coast of Ireland where I grew up, was like a wonderland. It was really remote and rugged. But when I reflect on that period of my life, it's not so much the village and surrounding area that stirs my imagination. It's the memory of the people.

When I think back now, a sea of faces comes to my mind. There was Nora Dan, the most wonderful human being you could ever hope to meet. When people talk about Nora Dan, it's with so much affection. Nora lived up at the graveyard, about two miles from me. She was a bit eccentric, but she loved people, and callers to her home were welcomed with open arms. The house couldn't be full enough for her. And, indeed, it wasn't only humans you'd find there. You'd often see the hens putting their heads through the door, and Nora's reaction would be, 'Shush! Who invited you for tea?'

I remember one day, Nora got involved in a discussion with my sister Kathleen about my future. There was great concern about what was going to become of me when I left school, because it was well known that I was absolutely useless with my hands. I might as well not have been born with hands – they were only there to finish off my arms. People in those days judged you by how you performed at manual tasks, working in the fields or in the bog cutting turf [sections of peat used as natural fuel]. As far as that kind of work was concerned, I was the village idiot. I couldn't master the simplest manual skill. So the big worry was, 'How's poor Daniel going to survive in the world at all, at all?'

'Well now, I don't know what you're going to do,' said Nora.

My sister Kathleen suggested: 'Maybe he'll go to the bank?'

'No,' said Nora, 'you wouldn't have laces in your shoes till you were a bank manager. And there are so few managers. You'd have to be a clerk and you'd have nothing. Well, now, maybe the Guards [police]?'

But Kathleen pointed out: 'Sure he has bad eyesight.'

'Oh,' said Nora, 'you need the sight. If you were over at the turn [bend on the road] and there was after being a robbery in the village, you'd need to be able to read the number of their car.'

Poor Nora was perplexed. She sauntered off, shaking her head. What was going to become of young Daniel?

Then there was John Phil, a huge, rotund, jolly man, much loved by everyone in the village. He was incredible, the unusual things he did. I really believe that if the Leaning Tower of Pisa hadn't been built, he would have got around to doing it. For instance, he was a big, big man and he bought a Mini car. How he ever got into it is beyond me. He used to travel everywhere in second gear and you'd hear him coming miles away. John was very self-sufficient. He liked to fish and I recall how he used to make flies out of the feathers from hens. There was no such thing as a Black & Decker drill in those days: whenever John Phil needed to bore a hole, he put a poker in the fire and when it was red hot he'd run out the door with it to the area where he was working!

There was Pat Neil Pat, who had a big house in the village and seemed to be involved in everything. He was the harbour master and he had houses for rent. I remember he had a big car, which was really rare in those days. And he always drove at his own pace, maybe ten or fifteen miles an hour, no matter where he'd be going. I recall that on one occasion when the politician Neil Blaney was canvassing in County Donegal, Pat took our neighbour Annie McGarvey and myself with him in the car to hear Blaney's oration. We followed the politician's cavalcade around the county, but by the time we arrived in each town, Blaney was finishing his speech! We never did get to hear that speech, but there was no way that Pat would drive any faster.

Annie lived next door to us with her father, Josie McGarvey, who was the village blacksmith (as I mentioned, we drew water from their well). She had a cow, a donkey called Johnny and hens. She was like family to me. When I was a young schoolboy, if Annie was sick I'd put Johnny in the shed in the evening; I'd take in the eggs and the turf for the fire and I'd do her messages [shopping]. Annie used to have a pit of tatties [potatoes] out in the field and in the wintertime she'd cover them with hay to protect them from the frost. She was the only one living near us who had hay, and the making of hay down in the field was a big day. It wouldn't be a day's work now with the new machinery, but it was then.

Those were the kind of people who figured in my childhood. They weren't hip. They weren't trendy types. They were plain, ordinary, unpretentious folk who lived at a much slower pace than we do today.

It was a tough life, but there was a great spirit of neighbourliness, with people helping other people whenever the need arose. They had their own fund of stories. They created their own fun. And so many of them were such colourful characters.

This was the life and the community that I was born into. If I hadn't made my name as a singer, I'd still be known at home as Daniel Bosco. Growing up, we were known as the Bosco family. That name distinguished us from the other O'Donnells living in the area. My eldest brother is called John Bosco. It's a common feature in our neck of the woods where there are numerous families bearing the same surname. Letters would arrive at our house with just the name Bosco written on the envelope. The post would reach its destination without a hitch because we were the only Boscos living in the locality.

My father, who came from Acres, near Burtonport, County Donegal, was Francie O'Donnell, but he and his family were known as the Donie Owens. I know the nicknames sound very confusing to outsiders, but they actually worked very well. His father's name was Daniel, and I'm called after my grandfather. My father's mother was Kitty Duffy, but she was known as Kitty Johnny Jondie because there were so many Duffys. She married Donie Owen and they had eleven children, my father being the second youngest and the seventh son.

Being the seventh son, he had the cure of something they called 'the evil'. It was some kind of lump that people developed on their bodies and he could cure it with special prayers. He cured several neighbours in his day.

My grandfather on my mother's side was James McGonagle. And my grandmother was Margaret Sharkey, known as Margaret Neddy. They lived just off the Donegal coast on the little island of Owey, where my mother came from. My grandfather died in 1963, so I don't remember him. But I was very close to my grandmother because she lived with us when I was growing up.

When my parents met for the first time, it certainly wasn't in the most romantic circumstances. Their first encounter was at the guttin'. And that wasn't the name of a dancing venue. They were both working at the dreadful task of cleaning out the entrails of fish at Lerwick in the Shetland Islands, off Scotland. In those days it wasn't easy to eke out a living and you took whatever work was going. It was an awful life, but they made the most of it and they had good times too, judging by the stories that were told.

Love blossomed between my parents and they married a year later, in 1948. I've always found it strange the way fate works. Burtonport to Owey Island is only four miles to the shore and then fifteen minutes on a currach. And they went all the way to the Shetland Islands before they met!

They had five children: John, Margaret (Margo), Kathleen, James and yours truly. I was born on 12 December 1961, in the local Dungloe Hospital. Wasn't that a great day for the world!

My brother John, the eldest in the family, is thirteen years older than me. John has worked in many careers throughout his life, including a fish processing plant, a bakery and even as a driver for our sister Margaret during the early days of her career. He lives in Burtonport with his wife,

Brigid. They have two sons, Frankie and Joey. Kathleen and her husband, John Doogan, reared four lovely children, John Francis, Patricia, Fiona and Daniel. They live in Kincasslagh in what was originally the house where I grew up. It was redesigned and rebuilt many years ago.

Margaret, who is better known as Margo, became a household name in Ireland as a singer, long before anyone had heard of me. She's just over ten years older than me and, like myself, she loves the stage and still performs today.

James, who is just four years older than me, is involved in a Dublin bar, Cassidy's of Camden Street, and I think everyone knows him because he's such a character. He's married to Eileen and they have three children, Paul, Chris and Margaret. He's well known in GAA circles, especially the Gaelic football scene, and has a great knowledge of the sport.

As emigration was very much an enforced facet of Irish life in those days, as it is today, there were very few teenagers or young adults in our village when I was growing up. Once people reached a certain age, they all left home in search of work abroad. So, the people in my childhood were all very old.

Because we were the only house in the village where an island woman lived – as I said, my mother came from Owey – the islanders from Owey used to stay overnight with us whenever they came to the mainland. The men from Tory Island would also spend their nights with us. Eamon and Anton were two old men who called regularly and they'd sleep in a sitting position on chairs by the open fire. There was no limit to the number of people who would come to stay in our home. They'd roast fish – mackerel and herring – over the fire and there were always great sing-songs.

Like most youngsters from the country, I had a number of pets to play with as a child. We had cats and a series of dogs, of course, but I also had a rabbit and a pigeon called Jacko. He was a wild pigeon and I clipped his wings so he couldn't fly. Wasn't that an awful thing to do! The rabbit was a wee white one and he was lovely. The whole lot of them used to sleep around the fire, including the pigeon. As he couldn't fly, he had nowhere else to go! So the dog and the cats and the pigeon and the rabbit all slept together in harmony, they were so used to one another. I loved pets at that time, but now I've become allergic to many living things like that.

We had a dog called Rover who used to go away on the ram-dam [the hunt] after lady dogs. He'd be away for a couple of days, then he'd return, literally with his tail between his legs. That was always a wild day as he'd get battered by my mother who had been worried and was hoping she'd teach him to stay at home. He'd know he was in for it too, because he'd be crying coming up the hill to our house. He'd come in looking sheepish, his head hanging low, knowing full well what was in store for him.

Mother would be out, calling: 'Where were you?'

And our John would say: 'Tell her, Rover! Tell her!'

One time he was away for so long that when he came back he was as thin as a whistle. But he got a great *fáilte* [welcome] that day because everyone in the family was so relieved to see him alive and well. We had all feared the worst because he was gone for so long. Rover didn't know what was happening with all the excitement going on around him, because he was expecting the usual trouncing! He was a mongrel, part sheepdog, and we all adored him, despite his wayward habits.

As the youngest in the family, I was never far away from my mother most of the time, but whenever she wanted to slip off without me, she used to say, 'You can't come with me, Daniel. I'm going to confession.'

I always accepted that excuse and never kicked up a fuss. But, subconsciously, I must have realised that she was trying to pull a fast one on me, because one day I was going up the road and Rover was tagging along. I didn't want him with me, so I turned back to my mother and shouted, 'Mammy, tell Rover I'm going to confession!'

It's funny how a child's mind works.

Eventually, Rover died from old age on the very same day our James was bringing home a new addition to the family – a wee white terrier. Rover died half-an-hour before the terrier arrived. That's the truth. There was a wild bit of crying altogether when poor Rover passed on. We, of course, then called the terrier Rover.

The terrier needed a haircut every so often, because he was always messing around in ditches and picking up dirt. My mother would then give him some kind of tablets to sedate the poor mutt while the grooming operation was being performed. But this night, anyway, she went through the usual procedure and sure poor Rover never woke up. He had died from an overdose. He was then only about three months old. I was very upset and ordered everyone to clear off!

That death finished it – there were no more dogs in our house after that.

We had some lovely cats, but there was one big red tomcat and he'd nearly eat you. We couldn't catch him. He was completely wild. My mother did everything to try and kill him. He even got his foot run over by some sort of farm machinery and he ended up with only half a leg, but he still survived. I must admit, I wasn't very fond of that cat myself. He was horrible, to be honest.

One day, a neighbour, Mary Hugo, was crying about all her cats.

'And what happened to them?' my mother asked.

'I'll tell you what happened now,' sobbed poor Mary. 'There was whiskey poured into the milk in the cats' dish and the cats all died.'

Well, my mother couldn't wait to get home to get the whiskey bottle out. But do you think it killed our one? Not at all. He only thrived. Mind you, he disappeared shortly after that. He either got the message or he met a fate that I was never told about.

My playground as a child also included Owey Island. I spent my holidays there as a youngster, running wild. One abiding memory is that the sun always shone on the island in the mornings. There was no rain that I can remember.

Fishing was the main occupation carried on there and I can recall the men going out in the early hours of the morning – you'd hear the sound of wellington boots on the gravel. A wellington boot makes a different noise to a shoe, and I can still hear that sound – the wellington army off to the fishing. I never went with them. I didn't like the sea. I was always kind of afraid of it. But I loved that island. There was a wonderful silence on it. It was another world.

It's an uninhabited island today, but way back then, my granduncle Andy lived there with his wife Ellen and son Neilie. Andy was the postman, then Neilie became the postman when he retired. I also used to stay there with my Uncle James and his wife, Peggy. There were only two families on the island that we weren't related to, so we were all *muintir* [the one people]. I'd spend my days swimming and playing with the other kids, especially Mary McGonagle, my cousin, who was two years older than me, and John Martin, who was a bit younger.

I remember, too, the dances in the school on Owey. It was like a scene from the old TV show *Little House on the Prairie*. If there was a party it was held in the school too. One such function I recall there was for my mother's cousin, Dominic McDevitt, when he returned home from America for a short holiday.

Whenever an emigrant came home from the USA, everyone on the island turned out to meet the boat. At the time, there were up to a hundred people living on Owey – each family had ten or twelve children. And when someone was leaving the island for the States, every man, woman and child went down to the boat to see them off. I remember the great sadness that fell over the community when people were going away. The pain of emigration for families is terrible, and it's awful to see that it still goes on to this day.

On the mainland where I lived, one of the biggest outings was to the bog (peatland) for the cutting of the turf, which we used for fuel. I hated the bloody auld bog, but it was a grand day really. You'd get a lift up to it on a tractor, which was a big thrill way back then. And there'd be great feeds. Very often there'd be lemonade, which was a novelty at the time. I remember one house where the kids had Lucozade, Cidona and lemonade all the time and I thought they were really posh.

We didn't travel far from home in those days, but one time when we were small, my cousin James and his new bride Doreen came over on holidays. At the time, *The Sound of Music* was on in the cinema in Donegal town, or so we thought. James and Doreen decided to go up to Donegal to see it and they took us along. It was like going to America, even though it was only slightly over forty miles. We set off in the car: James and Doreen, Mammy, Kathleen, my brother James and myself. We weren't far on the road when our James got sick and vomited all over Mammy's new coat! Well, she clattered him at the side of the road. When we got there, *The*

Sound of Music wasn't on at all. Then our James demanded chips, and he after getting sick on the way up!

Before my father died, we often went to Derry on holidays during the summer. We stayed with a family friend called Leslie Harkin, down in Westland Street. That was a great treat for us kids. Even though I was very young, I can still remember that period vividly. I particularly recall the type of things that only kids remember, like the big park up beside the cathedral with its wonderful swings. That park was like Disneyland to us because we had no such attractions at home. The fun we had on those swings! We could happily have spent our young lives there. And I remember the man who used to come around in a van selling lemonade. He was like the Pied Piper, surrounded by kids clamouring for his goodies.

My grandmother, Margaret Neddy from Owey Island, lived with us up to the time she died in 1973. I remember I used to sleep with her when we moved to our new home. She was a grand old lady, a real old-style woman. She had white hair tied in a bun, wee glasses, long skirts and a shawl. She always dressed in black.

Granny regularly went back to visit her island home. Even on her ninetieth birthday she put on her wellington boots and was brought over on the small boat.

On that same occasion a friend, Biddy Tague, came over to visit her and I recall Granny showing Biddy what she was wearing and revealing that it was her wedding dress! It was a dark colour and she still had it. At the age of ninety!

CHAPTER 4

OFF TO SCHOOL

When I started school my teddy bear accompanied me on my first day. He was bigger than me, so he gave me moral support and I didn't get upset or lonely for home.

Our school, Belcruit National School, was just a two-room building. It was built in 1964, so it was fairly new when I started there in 1967. It was a mile and a half from home, which was a long walk for a wee child. In later years during the autumn months, the return journey often took me three hours because I'd stop to pick blackberries growing wild in the ditches along the meandering path.

My teacher almost all the way through school was Miss Gallagher, who later became Mrs Logue, and I don't think I ever gave her much trouble. I was always reasonably well behaved. But I suppose I got the odd scutch

[slap] when I deserved it. Miss Gallagher was a good teacher and I think I was fairly bright. I wasn't a genius, but I wasn't stupid either. I got on all right and I enjoyed the days there. I loved maths; it was my best subject and I always wanted to be ahead of the rest of the class. In particular, I loved algebra. Later on, I had notions of becoming an accountant, but they never came to anything.

I suppose the highlights of those early schooldays in Ireland are centred around the Roman Catholic religious ceremonies of First Communion and Confirmation. My First Communion in 1969 was a sad event because my father had died the previous year. I remember that having a bearing on it. The suit I wore had been worn by my brother John when he'd made his First Communion thirteen years previously. Nowadays when children make their First Communion it's a big family occasion, with meals out in restaurants and so forth. But I got ice cream in the village on the walk home from church, and that was my treat.

Confirmation is another special day in the life of a young Catholic boy. There was a big lead-up to it, as you had to learn the catechism in detail. Mrs Logue was obviously a very good teacher because I remember that on Confirmation day I actually thought something was going to physically happen to me: that I was going to experience something special. I watched my friends going up to the bishop and as they returned I was thinking: 'Oh God, he's got IT. She's got IT.' Then I went up myself and I got nothing, as I thought. But now, when I look back, I realise the importance of it as far as my religion is concerned.

The suit I wore on my Confirmation day was bought for me by my sister Margaret [Margo] and it was too big. In those days, there were no professional photographic sessions to capture the special occasion. Our neighbour, Annie McGarvey, took the photographs at my First Communion and Confirmation. She was our Patrick Lichfield, the famous British photographer. Whatever was to be recorded, she recorded it. Annie had photographs dating back to 1937, the year she first got her camera!

The summers in those days seemed to be endless. Looking back, they were such carefree days. We were so innocent. Life was simple – just wonderful, fun-filled days playing silly games like cowboys and Indians, with sticks for guns and bows and arrows. There were no high-tech toys at that time.

I've always been an easy-going guy – it takes a lot to freak me out over something. I'm probably like that by nature, but I also believe that one of the people who helped me to develop that laid-back approach to life was a lady called Mrs Ashforth, who was a native of County Mayo but lived in our area. My cousin, Mary McGonagle, and myself used to spend a lot of time up at Mrs Ashforth's house when we were teenagers. We did odd jobs for her, like cutting the grass. Mrs Ashforth had a great outlook on life. She loved the sun, just like myself today, and in the summertime she would bask in it all day long. Whenever she'd see people rushing around in the good weather, she'd always remark: 'There's one thing that will never go away and that's the dust. It will always wait on us.' She was implying that everything else will wait too. I remember thinking, 'How right she is.' And that attitude stuck with me to this day.

Christmas was a great time too. We lived on the Smith's Brae, so called because the blacksmith Josie McGarvey lived at the top of it. ('Brae' is the Scottish for hill, and there's a big Scottish influence in our locality because so many people worked in Scotland.) When it snowed we had such fun on our sleighs. We'd go right down the hill into the village, and if you were really good you'd make a turn and continue on down to the strand. At night time, we used to throw water on the brae to make sure it would be really slippy for the sleighs the following morning.

People at that time had a very casual attitude to injuries. A gash that nowadays would lead to all hell breaking loose in the family home, and a frantic trip to the doctor's surgery with the injured child, hardly raised an eyebrow during my childhood days. I suppose people had a fear of the doctor's surgery. Or perhaps they were just a tougher species then. They had probably become immune to cuts and bruises, which were a regular feature of daily life with so many people engaged in manual jobs.

A personal injury that has remained in my memory is the day I fell on the road and slashed my face. Sure, I thought I was killed! There was blood pumping out of my face and I thought the skin was hanging off. I couldn't understand why my mother was remaining so calm and me about to die, as I firmly believed. There was no ambulance called. And no doctor. The only 'surgery' performed was done by my mother when she rubbed butter into the wound. Butter had some great uses in those days. In this case, it was applied to remove the tar from the cut. I still have a facial scar from that incident. But you would hardly notice it now because the crow's feet, or laughter lines if you prefer, have joined up with it.

One Christmas, my friend Anne Sharkey, along with her sister and two other girls, decided that we would do the 'Mummers'. That's a local tradition in which people dress up in costume and go singing in the local houses and bars. Instead of singing, however, we decided to do a full Nativity play. And we made a lot of money – about £50 each, which was a fortune to us at that time. So every year after that, even when we were at secondary school [second level], we did the 'Mummers'. We'd do four or five nights and call to all the pubs. The customers would be full of the joys of life with the booze and they were extra generous to us as a result.

Of all the toys I ever got for Christmas, the one I remember most was a big red plastic bus, which had no moving parts. But I used to sit on it and pretend I was driving it, and I loved that red bus.

I always sang in the choir at midnight Mass on Christmas Eve, and that's something I still do to this day.

Nowadays, I'm not a great Christmas person. I love the ceremony that is midnight Mass, but I don't share the feeling that some people have for Christmas. It's not that I dislike it, but I don't build myself up for it like most people do. I love going to midnight Mass in Kincasslagh because it's the only time in the whole year when everyone seems to be together under the same roof. You look around and there's a sea of faces that you know. The emigrants are home from abroad and everyone is acknowledging each other with nods. It's a very special occasion. Our chapel is close to the shore and when you go down to Mass on Christmas Eve, it's a beautiful scene, particularly if the moon is out and the tide is in.

From about the age of nine, I worked in The Cope, a general store in the village. And I feel that The Cope, and the people it introduced me to, had a huge influence in shaping the person that I am today. It was my first introduction to dealing with people whom I had never met before. I was always very reserved – and still am in certain ways today – but working in The Cope gave me the ability to reach out, and it helped me to converse well with strangers.

The Cope was a store that had everything from animal feed to welling-ton boots and general household items and food. I started off sweeping the floor and weighing the corn, layers' mash, chick mash, and corn cake for the cows. They also had a van on the road, a travelling store selling to people who lived in outlying areas and, eventually, I worked on that. For a lot of people who lived in that part of County Donegal, the Cope van would be their memory of me. That's how I became known to a lot of people around my area and its environs long before I made my name as a singer.

It was a good time for me. I loved going out on the van. People would invite you into their home for tea. Betty Doogan's, I recall, was one place where we always got something to eat – the fish fingers, in particular, I remember so well. On other days when I did relief work in another Cope in nearby Annagry, I'd get my dinner in Biddy the Butcher's and the dessert would always be arctic roll, which was sponge cake with ice cream in the middle. Delicious!

While working on the van, I met Protestants for the first time. I grew up at a time when there was no real contact between Protestants and Catholics. There was a lot of ignorance about each other's way of life. For instance, I had this impression that Protestants wouldn't like country music because I liked it. And the first time I went into a Protestant church, I thought that there would be some kind of terrible consequences – I was afraid to stand up in case I'd be struck dead or deformed! I thought I'd be condemned to hell for going in. But in I went anyway and sure didn't I live to tell the tale. Nothing happened of any consequence. The Protestants I met on the van, the Boyds, opened my eyes to the fact that they were just the same as me.

I continued working in The Cope every summer, until I was fourteen. I also worked there for two hours every evening after school and all day Saturday. My wages at the end of the week were £2 and I saved the money for my annual holiday to Scotland. I travelled over on my own by boat – wasn't I a very brave young lad! – and I stayed with relatives in Glasgow,

Edinburgh, Perth and Callander. When I perform in Edinburgh nowadays, I often remember the cuckoo clock in Prince's Street Gardens. As a kid I used to be mesmerised by the cuckoo coming out of the clock on the hour. A crowd always gathered to watch it and it took me a long time to discover that it was a mechanical cuckoo. Up to then, I always thought it was real!

I liked shopping in Edinburgh and was always on the lookout for a bargain. On one occasion, I bought two pairs of shoes with gold tips on the toes. I thought I was a real dandy and couldn't wait to show them off in the village when I got back. Sunday Mass provided me with a great opportunity, so off I strutted on my first weekend home. I was proudly putting each foot forward, hoping that people would notice.

Coming out of the church, a fella said to me, 'You have a fine pair of shoes on.'

'Do you like them?' I asked, as proud as punch.

'You got a quare bargain at £4.99,' he smirked.

The sale sticker was still on the sole of the shoe and everyone had seen it when I knelt at the altar for Communion. I was so embarrassed when I made this terrible discovery.

I stayed in national school till I was in seventh class. I was man big. Then I went up to Dungloe for my second-level education. Dungloe secondary school was amalgamated with the technical school in Loughanure and you had to attend the Tech, as it was known, for the first year. The secondary school was more academic, whereas the Tech covered practical subjects like woodwork.

By the time the year was up, I had become friendly with P.J. Sweeney and Patrick Kyles. They were very good with their hands and excellent at the practical subjects. Because they were staying on in the Tech part of the school, 'muggins' decided to stay on too, even though I was useless with my hands and hated woodwork. I was also useless at science and mechanical drawing. I was just hopeless at those subjects and I had no interest in them.

Poor Cundy, he was a retired headmaster who was teaching woodwork. I remember one day I made a dovetail joint and I thought it was fairly good. All the good joints used to be put on display. And I thought this was a real humdinger. So, Cundy inspected the joint and then handed it back to me.

I said to him, thinking it was heading for the mantelpiece, 'What'll I do with it now, Sir?'

And he came over really close to me and said, 'Throw it in the fire.'

But the Tech in Loughanure was great all the same. Cassie's shop was nearby and we all trooped down there in the middle of the day. We used to buy sweets and eat them sitting around the fire. Anne Sharkey was my best friend at school. And if Anne and her classmates were doing cookery during domestic science classes, I'd go in and join them. I had this way with me that I could get in through the eye of a needle. I shouldn't have been in there, but Miss Keady, their teacher, turned a blind eye. So, I'd be in with the girls, eating what they cooked.

Miss Breslin was our book-keeping teacher. She wore a headscarf and had her own inimitable style about her. She would sit at her desk peering down at us, chanting: 'Draw a red line, skip a blue line. Draw a red line, skip a blue line ...' It became her sort of catchphrase and even to this day, whenever people from her class meet, they go: 'Draw a red line, skip a blue line ...'

P.J., Patrick and myself were good at the book-keeping and we were the only boys in the class. Miss Breslin used to say to the girls, 'It's a wonder ye wouldn't be like these three fellas up here!' We were her pride and joy.

Although we didn't know it at the time, she used to smoke. Her book-keeping class was a double class, so she'd leave the room for a quick puff in the middle of it. One day she went out and left her scarf behind her.

I went up to her desk, put on her scarf and began mimicking her: 'Draw a red line, skip a blue line ...'

Well, didn't she come back and catch me at it! She walked up to the desk and stood there stony-faced while I took off the scarf and went back to my desk. She sat down and never said a word. But she didn't have to. The shame of being caught making fun of a woman who thought I was a saint was enough punishment.

In the wintertime, when I was in secondary school, I used to hate getting up on the cold mornings to head off on the early bus. I'd stick my head out from under the blankets and see the steam from my breath almost freezing before my eyes in the bedroom. A glance at the window would reveal that 'Jack Frost' had arrived. There was no central heating in the houses in those days and no electric blankets. At that time, only my mother and I were in the house. I always got up, prepared my own breakfast and got myself out to school. But occasionally I just wouldn't have the motivation to go in and I'd say to my mother, who'd still be in bed, 'There's snow today!'

And she'd say, 'Oh, if it's a bad day, maybe you shouldn't bother going.'

Well, I'd be back under those warm blankets like lightning.

By the time my mother got up there wouldn't even be a trace of frost on the ground, and she'd throw me a quizzical look.

'Ah sure, the snow thawed out,' I'd explain.

Amazingly, I always got away with that stunt.

The second-level school was a good time for me. I got on well with all the teachers. In our fourth year, we went to France. That was a wonderful experience. It was in 1979 and that was an amazing adventure for me at the time – from Donegal to France! We went on the boat from Rosslare to Le Havre. I remember we were singing all the time on the Metro in Paris. It was the year Cathal Dunne represented Ireland in the Eurovision Song Contest with 'Happy Man'.

And we were all singing 'Happy Man'.

During my schooldays, I got many opportunities to show off my singing talents in the local community. I loved being in the limelight and I never needed any encouragement to sing for an audience.

One entertainment event that introduced me to the stage in those days was the local variety concert, which was staged in the parish hall. Those concerts, scripted and performed by people in the community, provided hours of live entertainment. And they unearthed the many hidden talents of neighbours, who impressed all and sundry with their acting, singing and musical skills.

The variety concert was a great tradition, with people staging their home-produced shows in small towns and villages throughout the land before the advent of television. They united young and old and gave people, particularly teenagers, the confidence that comes from performing in public. Lots of people around the country met their partners through such productions I'm sure, because they brought together people whose lives might not have crossed otherwise. They were a real asset to the community.

When I was a youngster, there were always dances in the village hall on a Sunday afternoon. Rose Marie Brennan, an aunt of members of the Irish group Clannad and of Enya, was the resident entertainer. She sang and played the accordion. The adults danced the soles off their shoes while the children caused havoc chasing each other around the dancefloor.

When I was in my teens the big sporting event every Sunday was the regatta. The skiff races were really exciting and involved the entire community. I wasn't part of the team, but I was a great supporter. Our team was one of the best, so they won a lot of big events. The support they received at competitions around the country was fantastic – two hundred people often travelled with them to cheer them on.

The céilí [traditional dancing] was another great form of entertainment in our area. It was much more enjoyable than an ordinary dance because you could get up with anyone in a 'set' without asking. There was also a great tradition of having tea at the céilí, which gave people the opportunity to sit and chat together.

At school, although I had friends, I was a bit of a loner. I never really liked playing football. And I was the kind of individual who wouldn't do something I didn't like just because everyone else was doing it. As a result, I used to get a lot of slagging. People used to ask me in the early days of my career, 'How do you put up with all the slating you're subjected to?' Sure I grew up dealing with it – and I still dislike some of my fellow students as a result of it. I was soft and they gave me such a hard time. They called me a sissy because I'd get up to let some old person have a seat on the bus. They laughed at me for that kind of thing. If you weren't involved in causing trouble, you'd be called a sissy. Maybe it was also due to the fact that I spent more time with Anne Sharkey than I did with fellas. I suppose that's something that's difficult to understand. But as I grew older I realised that it can happen with a lot of people, that their friend can be a girl – and just be a friend. I think everyone thought that Anne and I would eventually get married.

Anne was a year ahead of me at school, so we weren't in the same class.

But whenever I had a free class, I'd slip into Anne's classroom to join her and her friends and we'd have a great laugh. I was good craic [fun], or so they used to tell me, and I'd have all the gossip, which is funny because today I have no time for people who like to gossip about others. I suppose as I grew older I developed a different perspective. But, looking back, it wasn't malicious gossip or anything like that, it was just harmless fun.

So, because I hung out with the girls I came in for a really hard time from some of the lads in the school. And I would never stand up for myself. I'd run a mile rather than fight. I hated swearing and I never used swear words. Nowadays, I let out an odd *focal mór*, as we called the swear words, but I never cursed in those days. So I was seen then as being 'Mr Perfect'.

I didn't do well in my Leaving Certificate [Irish equivalent of the O and A Levels]. I didn't really work at school in my last year or so. I worked for the teachers whom I thought were good. I thought I was working for them when, in fact, I should have been working for myself. I think all children are like that. It's not till you get older that you realise you should have been putting in the effort for yourself. I always hated exams and I never performed well at them. They made me nervous and I could never concentrate.

My best subject was accountancy – but I'll never forget that exam. I just freaked out. I still feel that there should be some different form of assessment on your performance over a number of years, rather than what you produce in exams over a few hours. I did honours [higher level] in English, Irish, accountancy and economics. I only got the honour in economics, but I passed everything and it was a good enough Leaving Cert to get me into Galway Regional College, the next level of my education.

I had no idea then where my life was going and I certainly didn't foresee what lay ahead.

CHAPTER 5

A MOTHER'S LOVE

I was only six years old when my father, Francie, died from a heart attack at the age of forty-nine. Naturally, this was a very traumatic time in our family, but being so young it didn't have the same devastating impact on me as it did on my older siblings. And I can't even imagine our poor mother's pain in that bleak period of our family history.

My father had spent most of his married life working in Scotland and sending home the money to support his wife and children back in Kincasslagh. That was the reality for so many families, as there was little work to be had in our area.

Because I was so young when my father died and due to him being away for long periods after I came into the world, I have little memory of him. I only know him through other people.

Dad's life had been one of separation and hardship. He did hard, manual work, employed in fish processing and on farms around Scotland as a labourer. It is so far removed from the privileged life that would come my way.

One of my vivid memories of my father is that when he came home I would be put out of the bed I shared with my mother at the time. The routine of a child is not one to be tampered with, so I was none too pleased with that I can tell you!

By all accounts, my father was a saintly man. He was a man of prayer. And people used to come and ask him to pray for them. Being a seventh son, as I mentioned, gave him healing powers and he was known for possessing this gift.

When she later wrote her own life story, my mother recalled the dark days surrounding my father's death. Mother said that no words could describe the pain in our house on the day of the funeral.

'The wailing of the children would have melted the hardest of hearts,' she wrote. 'Poor little Daniel didn't really know what was going on, but he became very upset when he saw the coffin leaving the house. Daniel clung to it and cried, 'Don't youse take me daddy away. Bury him in the garden.'

'He held my hand and pleaded, 'Please, Mammy, don't let them take our dad away, we need him here at home.' He kept crying, 'Everyone will have a daddy now but us.' Then he asked, 'Will Dad ever come back?''

My mother said she then told me that Dad wouldn't be coming home as God wanted him and we had to let him go.

She also recalled that in the days of my father's funeral as she was trying to get the family back to work and school, I was determined to stay at home with her.

'I can't go, Mammy, you will be lonely without Dad,' I cried and cried.

Mam was a very strong woman and she had to be because she had the responsibility of looking after five children after my father died. The eldest, John Bosco, was just nineteen at the time.

My mother has been the big influence in my life. I loved her dearly and I had tremendous admiration for the way she reared the family after our father died. It must have been a great struggle for her because my father never earned enough money to put by savings for a rainy day. So I don't think she had anything at all when he died. Whatever the widow's pension was – and it wasn't a lot – she paid the bills out of it. And she used to knit sweaters and send them to America. The money that came back helped to support the family, although my brother, John, and sister, Margaret, were then bringing home a wage too.

My mother was very good to all of us. Being the youngest, I was probably spoilt in a way. But I wasn't over-spoilt. I never grew up expecting much and I think that's all due to my mother. I never wanted for anything, but I was also cute enough not to look for things that I knew I couldn't get. I knew what the limitations were. Even to this day, I'm not motivated by money. The money is a by-product of what I've always wanted to do.

***

My mother was no stranger to struggle and hardship as she grew up in an era when hard labour was the order of the day. Her home on Owey Island was a two-bedroom cottage, which she shared with her parents and her sister and three brothers growing up.

Despite the austerity of those times, my mother felt blessed that she was born into a happy home with loving parents. Her schooling finished at the age of fourteen, and at fifteen it broke her heart when she was forced to leave Owey in order to find work on the mainland, going into service as a housekeeper with a family in Derry.

By the age of sixteen my mother had emigrated to Lerwick, one of the Shetland Islands off Scotland, where she got a job in the fishing industry. This entailed the gruelling task of being part of a crew gutting fish outdoors in a port in all kinds of weather conditions.

Later, Mother found work 'tattie howking' (potato picking) in Ayrshire, Scotland, where the sleeping quarters were a cowshed. 'After a long day working in the fields, the cowshed seemed the most welcoming place on earth,' she recalled.

As I mentioned, it was while working on a fish-gutting crew that she met my father, Francie, her future husband, at a Saturday night dance. 'He was a very handsome young man who had lovely brown hair with a wave through it, a strong physique and a great smile,' Mam remembered.

They got married in September 1948 when Mam was twenty-eight years old, and Dad a year younger. 'I suppose if it was today they'd be calling him my toyboy,' she joked during the telling of her own story.

Just a week after they tied the knot, the newlyweds were forced apart to find work, with my father going off to pull beet on a farm in Scotland while my mother secured employment in Great Yarmouth, England, packing herring. They wouldn't see each other again until Christmas.

'If I had one regret about my married life, it's the fact that I spent most of it separated from my lovely husband,' Mam said in later life.

My mother never wallowed in self-pity, even when she lost the love of her life. She got on with life and made the most of it. And she was so encouraging to her children to pursue their dreams. Mother loved music and singing and, as fate would have it, she ended up producing two professional singers and entertainers.

My sister Margaret, or Margo as she's known by her stage name, was the first to achieve success as a singer back in the 1960s. Margaret became one of Ireland's biggest entertainers and she had a huge influence on me. She is just over ten years older than me, and she started singing in a band when she was only twelve years old!

As a teenager, Margaret would travel home through the night in the back of a van from a dance and snatch a couple of hours sleep in the early morning before heading off to school. It was the true showbiz tradition of hard graft that got her to the top of her chosen career.

Growing up, I don't think I was conscious of the volume of her success. But I was aware that she was different to other kids' sisters. The first time I remember taking notice of her as a singer was in 1969, when I was only eight. She had a hit record with a song called 'Dear God', and it was played on the radio. I thought she was great.

As I grew older, I used to get away at weekends because my mother would travel to see her perform and she took me with her. It was on those occasions that I got my first taste of the stage, because Margaret would sometimes get me up to sing with her – I would have been nine, ten or eleven in those times.

When Margo became a household name throughout Ireland, our native county of Donegal was so proud of her achievement. Everyone in our area was delighted with her phenomenal success. The first time she had a No. 1 record, with a song called 'I'll Forgive and I'll Try To Forget', there were wild celebrations in the locality. That was in the early seventies and I

My father and mother,
Francis and Julia,
pictured in 1948, the
year of their wedding.

I was only a year old
when this photo was
taken, in 1962, and
someone obviously
thought I'd look better
wearing specs.

On the day of my Confirmation,
in 1972, when I was aged eleven.

Above: Posing with my mother in 1972.
Right: As a teenager, I was a member of the local Mullaghduff Fife & Drum Band. I carried the flag – that's how musical I was.

A family wedding. The bride was my sister Kathleen, who married John Doogan. They're pictured with my brothers John (extreme left) and James, and yours truly. In the front row are Brigid (John's wife), my mother Julia, Eileen (James's wife), Margaret, and my nephew Frankie.

An early photo session. Oh, how I hated having my photo taken!

Relaxing on the beach at home in Kincasslagh during a break from touring.

What a thrill! Here I am with country legend Dolly Parton and British TV and radio personality Gloria Hunniford.

At my TV special *Country Comes Home*, recorded in Dublin in 1989, I teamed up with some of the country scene's most talented performers, including Charley Pride and The Judds.

Performing with my idol, American country music legend Loretta Lynn, on *The Daniel O'Donnell Show*.

I've been a soccer fan since Donegal's Packie Bonner captured my imagination with his outstanding performance as a goalkeeper on the Republic of Ireland team in the 1990 World Cup.

Below left: Here I am with *The Late Late Show*'s Gay Byrne and Ireland's best-known priest, Fr Brian D'Arcy.

Below right: Standing by her man … Yours truly with Tammy Wynette.

Left: New York's famous Carnegie Hall: it's a long way from Kincasslagh, County Donegal! That 1991 concert is one I'll always remember.

Below: Touching hands at the Galtymore Ballroom in Cricklewood, London, in 1990.

Capturing the atmosphere in Nashville.

Thumbs up with top Nashville producer Allen Reynolds, who has also worked with Garth Brooks, Emmylou Harris, Don Williams and Crystal Gayle.

Here I am performing with Elvis Presley's backing band The Jordanaires at Fan Fair, the American showcase for country artists in Nashville.

Above: The Mullaghduff Fife & Drum Band, of which I was a member as a wee fella, making a presentation to me at home when I was awarded Irish Entertainer of the Year. **Below:** The big event of the year in my area – the Mary from Dungloe festival!

remember a cavalcade of cars turned out to meet her and there was a big party in the village hall. We had a great night, singing and dancing.

Another landmark in her career was the night she appeared on the *Late Late Show* for the first time. The Irish TV show, which was then hosted by Gay Byrne, is an institution. At the time, it was broadcast every Saturday night and I swear the streets and country roads were deserted while it was on. Certainly, anyone who had a television at that time was glued to the *Late Late Show* on a Saturday night. It was compulsive viewing. And appearing on the show with Gay Byrne was like appearing with God.

The night Margaret made her debut on the show was also cause for great celebration in our home upon her return from Dublin. All the neighbours came in and there was a big hooley. I remember her performance on the *Late Late* that night. She sang a song called 'The Bonny Irish Boy'. My father gave her that song before he died – he wrote it down and taught her the air. Margaret recorded it, but the day it was due out, our father died. He never heard that record.

Around that time, a guy called Hughie Green had a talent show on British TV called 'Opportunity Knocks'. My grandmother used to watch it and she was convinced that Hughie Green was waving at her. So convinced, in fact, that she used to wave back at him! The night Margaret appeared on the *Late Late Show*, she told Granny to put on her best outfit. On her return from Dublin, Margaret was told what Granny had been wearing that night in front of the telly. When Margaret later described the outfit to her, Granny was astounded.

'Well, good God, that Hughie Green can see me after all,' she gasped.

I became more aware of Margaret's success as I grew older. And I was quite happy to be Margo's brother. It was a great perk. Margaret shared the rewards of her success with the family. She was very good to us. After Granny died, she sent Mammy and myself to America on a holiday. The year was 1973 and for me it was like going to the moon. I was only twelve years old. Boy, did I have a good time out there! Although we were there only for a few weeks, I came back with a 'Yankee' accent. We had relatives living in New Jersey, including my mother's sister, Maggie. The first night in Bayonne, a party was thrown in our honour and we were treated like celebrities. I sang for them and loved all the attention.

I remember being in awe of the fact that everything in America was so vast compared to home. The roads had lane after lane and there were cars and lights everywhere. That's something I wasn't used to then. I couldn't get over the fact that the buildings in New York went up into the sky and were touching the clouds, as I thought. And when you went out onto the streets you'd never see anybody you knew. That was strange for me, because I knew everybody at home.

There must have been no Pepsi-Cola at home at that time, because I remember Pepsi-Cola and me, we had a great affair when I was in America. And the ice cream was just delicious.

That trip was a real dream. We came back with a mountain of gifts – a family of ten wouldn't have the amount of luggage we were carrying. Everything that was given to us, my mother took home. You couldn't see us behind the trolleys. It's just as well that they weren't charging for baggage back then or Mother would have had to remortgage the family home to pay for them!

On the way home from the airport, we stopped in Killala, County Mayo, where Margaret was performing at a carnival dance, and I got up to sing with her. I often went down to Killala on holidays to Martin Ford's pub.

Martin used to take me out in the car and I'd sing in loads of pubs that we visited. We went to Belmullet one night to see Margaret perform in a venue called The Palm Court and I got up to sing with her that night, too. 'Little Cabin Home on the Hill' and 'The Philadelphia Lawyer' were my songs. That was all great experience for me. It was my introduction to the live music scene and I took to it like a duck to water.

And that was Margaret's influence. Later, when I became established in my own right, Margaret and I recorded a duet together and it went to No. 1 in the Irish hit parade.

The song was called 'Two's Company', and to this day we are the only brother and sister ever to have had a No. 1 hit record in Ireland.

CHAPTER 6

FROM THE GRAVEYARD TO THE STAGE

Although I never had what people would term a 'proper' job after I left college, I was employed in some rather strange occupations during the summers leading up to my entry into the world of showbiz. I spent one summer working in a graveyard! I suppose you could call that a dead-end job! Well, you have to start somewhere.

I once heard that Rod Stewart was a gravedigger in his early days. If that's true then I'm in good company. But I didn't have to dig graves: my task was to maintain the graveyard. I always hated that kind of work and spent most of my time sunbathing behind the headstones.

I worked in Logue's store in the town of Dungloe for several weeks during another summer. I also secured employment on a local scheme, digging drains. I hated every minute of that. It was like working on a chain gang. That was in 1979 and the following year I progressed to washing dishes in Dublin's Central Hotel after completing my Leaving Certificate examination and leaving secondary school.

The summer of 1980 was a great period in my life. My brother James, who lives in Dublin, got me that job in the Central Hotel, where he also worked. And it was there that I met two women who became great friends – Margaret Coyle and Maura Cullinane. We were inseparable. I laughed my way through that whole summer. We really did have a ball, dancing every night in the Dublin clubs: The Ierne, The National, The Irish Club, The TV Club and The Olympic. These were mostly frequented by people from rural Ireland who were working in the capital. And they all featured the type of music that I enjoy. All the big names of the day were playing those venues at the time: Big Tom, Larry Cunningham, Philomena Begley, Brian Coll and my own sister, Margo.

The Irish Club was my favourite. There was a great buzz in it and I loved the formal-style dances: the waltzes, the quick-steps and the jives. I was never into disco dancing. Perhaps people might find it difficult to comprehend, but none of us got romantically involved. We went out together, we danced and had a laugh. And it never progressed beyond that.

I disliked the hotel work in the beginning because I was down in the lower kitchen, washing the pots and pans. But the situation improved when

I was promoted to the upstairs kitchen, which involved washing the plates and cutlery. The main advantage was that it was just off the dining room and you felt you were closer to the action. I remember one night there was a mouse in the dining room while customers were eating and I was sent out to discreetly catch it with a brush and pan. And me dead scared of mice! I never completed the mission as the little guy escaped through a crack or a hole somewhere in the room.

Because I wasn't working in the dining room, I didn't get the opportunity to meet the clientele. But one day a guest came into the kitchen and handed me £2 cash as a tip. She was staying in the hotel with mime artiste Marcel Marceau's entourage and she had heard me singing in the kitchen as I washed the dishes. She told me I was the happiest dishwasher she had ever heard!

Maura Cullinane, who was a waitress in the hotel, had a car and one day I persuaded her to take me down to Galway so that I could apply for a place in the Regional College. It wasn't her day off, so she made an excuse and told them she was going to a wedding. Margaret was on a day off, so she came too. I did the interview and got my place in the college. On the way back we bought a paper and I discovered that the Rose of Tralee festival was on in County Kerry. It was the final night of the event. We looked at each other ... and the next instant we were on the road to Kerry.

We had a wonderful evening in Tralee. I remember being smitten by the Jersey Rose – I thought she was gorgeous. We drove back to Dublin through the night and Maura had to put her head out the window to stay awake while driving. I got to bed at 6.30 that morning and I had to be up at 7.30 to get the bus to work. On the journey in to the hotel I thought I was going to throw up, I was so tired.

That was also the summer I learned how to drive. Maura taught me in her little blue Ford Fiesta. She let me drive from Dublin to Glendalough in County Wicklow one day. And I not fit to drive, no more than the cat. I had no insurance or anything. But that was a good summer for me. Poor Maura is no longer with us; she was a lovely girl. She died in 1992. I'm still very friendly with Margaret and I attended her wedding in 1992. That's something I'm very pleased about, the fact that the people I knew before my career took off are still part of my life today and they still want me in their lives. I'm glad that never changed.

***

In the autumn of 1980, I set off to Galway city to take up my place in the Regional College. My course was in business studies and my long-term plan was to eventually transfer to university. I had decided at one stage that I wanted to be a teacher. And if my passion for the stage hadn't made me change my direction, I think I would have been a reasonably good teacher. I'm fairly relaxed and hard to ruffle. I'm also very good at communicating with people and that's another reason why I thought I might teach. However, I didn't get enough points for university in my Leaving Cert, so I was using the Regional College as a stepping stone. It would have taken a bit longer. But sure I had all the time in the world. I was only eighteen.

My time in Galway Regional College turned out to be the unhappiest period of my life. I never settled and I was really miserable. I never socialised in the college. I had nothing in common with that kind of life or the people there. To this day, I still have no friends from the period I spent there. The friends I made during that era were from outside the college, in particular Sean and Pat Nugent, the family I was staying with. They made me feel really at home and a part of their clan.

Pat said, 'Wouldn't you be better off learning something first?' when I broke the news to her that I was leaving college to become a singer.

They did their best to help me settle, but it was a lost cause. I was really homesick for Donegal. From early on, I started going into Galway city to buy the Donegal newspaper. The first time, I borrowed a push-bike from the Nugents. But I ended up walking most of the way because I had never cycled in traffic before and I was terrified. I might as well have been on a highway in the States.

In the early stages, I started going home to Kincasslagh every third weekend. It was a gruelling journey that took hours and hours. The bus used to take me up to Donegal town, then I'd have to hitch the remaining forty-three miles to Kincasslagh. But even if Kincasslagh had been on another planet I wouldn't have cared. I would still have made the trek. In the end, I was doing that journey every weekend. So, the writing was on the wall.

Coming up to Christmas of that year, my sister Margaret was performing in Galway and I went to see her in the Galway Ryan Hotel where she was staying. I told her I wanted to leave college and become a singer. She advised me to think about it over Christmas. Margaret still recalls how I sent her a Christmas card that year and on it I wrote: 'Remember what I told you? I want to sing NOW!' And I underlined the word 'now'.

I did think about it over Christmas, and the more I thought about it the more convinced I became about joining Margaret in the world of show-business. I just knew in my heart and soul that it was where I wanted to be. Call it naievity or just plain ignorance at the time, but I really believed I could be a professional entertainer.

Not everybody was as certain about this as I was. Irish country star Philomena Begley was, and still is, one of my all-time favourite singers. If I was putting favourite country singers in order, I would place Philomena next to Loretta Lynn. So I decided to go and have a chat with Philomena about my own dream of becoming an entertainer.

Philomena was baking bread when I arrived at her home and had flour up to her elbows. Many years later she would tell me that she looked like Vera Duckworth of *Coronation Street* that day, because she had a head full of curlers. She was getting the hair done to sing at a dance that night. We engaged in some small talk before I eventually plucked up the courage to tell her of my burning ambition.

There was silence for what seemed like an eternity. Philomena just looked at me with an expression that screamed: 'Are you mad?'

Eventually Philomena spoke. 'Would you not be better sticking to the books, Daniel?' she asked me.

It wasn't what I wanted to hear. I wanted Philomena to tell me that I was absolutely making the right decision. I was so deflated, but it didn't really matter as I had my mind made up anyway.

On reflection, I know that Philomena's advice was sound. She knew how difficult it is to achieve success in the music business and how hard a life it can be. Philomena didn't have a crystal ball and couldn't have foreseen how my singing career would turn out. So she was right to encourage me to finish my education.

As I said, my mind was made up.

I didn't go back to college.

***

The year 1981 was a new beginning for me. It was the start of something that has snowballed beyond my wildest expectations. Margaret had agreed that I could join her band. It's something I'll always be grateful to her for. Getting a start is always the most difficult aspect of anything you want to do. I was lucky – I had my sister to turn to. So she found a place for me in her group.

On 28 January 1981, I stepped out on stage at a venue called The Ragg, in Thurles, County Tipperary. I was on rhythm guitar, but it wasn't plugged in, because I couldn't play a note! Isn't that dreadful? But sure I had to start somewhere. And if playing a 'dead' guitar was going to kick off my career, then I had no problem with that.

Some people start by cleaning offices in Nashville, washing floors or waiting on tables. Maybe standing on a stage with a guitar that's not plugged in isn't as honest as washing floors or waiting on tables, but it gave me the start. I'm sure the other band members must have thought I was a bit of a flute. Anyway, I stuck with it.

The guitar, incidentally, belonged to Margaret and she had never learned how to play it either. I had gone to guitar classes, but my heart was never in it. I think I had decided in my mind that if I ever mastered the guitar, I would always be left in the background and I'd never make it out to centre stage as a singer. That first night walking out on stage was a tremendous feeling. I was really excited and a bit giddy. It was wonderful. I was on my way. I felt like Engelbert Humperdinck.

Working with Margaret and her band gave me a wonderful insight into the live music business. It was great experience for me. I saw a lot of things that were good. But I also observed a side of the business that I didn't like, such as boozing into the early hours of the morning after a show. There were a lot of things like that that I wouldn't be interested in. And I do believe that what I witnessed with Margaret has made me the way I am. Margaret has had a hard time in her own career because of an alcohol problem, which she has talked about publicly. And I knew I never wanted that to happen to me. So many people in this business become victims to alcohol. It's one of the hazards of the scene. I never wanted to drink, and I think my mother was the main reason for that. She drummed it into us not to drink.

But on the positive side, I saw the joy that Margaret brought to people and how people admired her. And I wanted all those things too. Margaret allowed me to share the limelight on stage when she gave me a turn at the singing.

Eventually, I was performing seven or eight songs during the night. I suppose I always got a good response. But I remember one night in particular; it was in the St Francis Club in Birmingham, I sang 'My Donegal Shore' and I can still recall the applause. It was the first time that it really hit me. I knew then I was making an impression. It must have struck Margaret too, because she got me to sing a verse and chorus of the song again.

Inevitably, the time came for me to move on and spread my wings. I had to leave Margaret in order to progress.

My final performance as a member of my sister's band was in the Longford Arms Hotel in Longford town on 27 April 1983.

CHAPTER 7

'MY DONEGAL SHORE' AND A 'MIRACLE'

The song that started the ball rolling for me in my own career was 'My Donegal Shore'. That composition, written by a songwriter called Johnny McCauley, will always be close to my heart.

A native of Fahan, County Donegal, Johnny, who sadly died in 2012, was one of our great Irish songwriters, penning over eighty well-known songs including 'Destination Donegal', 'Among the Wicklow Hills', 'Pretty

Little Girl from Omagh' and 'Four Country Roads': the last of these being a big hit for Big Tom McBride.

Big Tom also recorded 'My Donegal Shore', long before me. But the first time it touched a chord with me was when I heard a girl called Bridie Cahill singing it unaccompanied.

While it was a slow burner for my career, once it took off it certainly was the power behind my early success. I recorded that song with my own money in Big Tom's studios in Castleblaney, County Monaghan, on 9 February 1983.

I was always a great saver, a real magpie. And I had accumulated just over £1000. It cost me £600 to record it on tape and it took another £600 to release it on record. That was the best money I ever spent.

My sister Kathleen and her husband, John, drove me up to Castleblaney that day and in the evening I left with a little tape that had four tracks on it: 'My Donegal Shore', 'Stand Beside Me', 'London Leaves' and 'Married by the Bible' (that one never escaped at all!).

In the studio that day, I remember thinking: 'What am I doing here? What do these people think of me?' I suppose I was insecure at the time. I knew why I was doing it, but I didn't really know what I was doing. I do remember the fella who was producing it – Basil Hendricks, an English musician living in Ireland – saying, 'That chap can sing.'

I opted for 'My Donegal Shore' and 'Stand Beside Me' on the record and I put it out on Margaret's label. I then sold every one of those records myself. I sold them anywhere and everywhere. I even sold them on a pilgrimage to Knock shrine in County Mayo, where the Blessed Virgin once appeared. I sang on the bus all the way down and all the way back and the pilgrims bought the records from me.

Annie McGarvey bought one and she didn't even have a record player! In all, I had a thousand records and I sold all of them and that covered my costs. I also sought a few people's advice on it. One of the individuals I approached was a country music radio critic. His comment was, 'Well, it's nice, but there's nothing spectacular about it.' I was disgusted by his reaction. Some time later, I met him coming out of a bank in Dublin's College Green and I was tempted to confront him and give him a piece of my mind. I was so determined to make it that anybody who didn't say, 'Yes, you can do it,' I pushed aside. I almost hated them. Nothing and nobody was going to get in my way.

Scotland was my first attack. I had friends in Glasgow – Kathleen and Eugene Sweeney. Whenever I stayed with them, they used to take me down to The Claddagh Club, The Irish Centre and The Squirrel Bar. Invariably, I got up to sing in those venues. So, when I brought out the record, I went over in May and it was arranged with the owners or managers of the venues that I could sing and that we could sell my records, which I brought along in a hold-all. I sang the songs that were on the single and Kathleen sold them to the audience.

I went down so well that the three venues invited me back to sing with their resident band. So I went back to Glasgow for a weekend and that was the first time I was advertised as a singer in my own right.

And once I got my name up in lights, I never took it down!

In July 1983, I got my first band together: Daniel O'Donnell and Country Fever. It featured Patrick Gallagher and Peter Healy (later a member of an Irish band, Goats Don't Shave), Dim Breslin and Joe Rogers, all of whom were from my area.

Our first night was in The Ostan Hotel in Dungloe. I'll never forget it.

I had the whole repertoire sung by 1 a.m. and we were booked to play till 2 o'clock in the morning. So, I started the first number again and off we went singing the same set of songs again.

We continued playing around our own area. When bands are starting off, members come and go, and we were no exception. Patrick Gallagher and Dim Breslin left and my friend P.J. Sweeney joined, along with Joe Rogers and his brother Peter.

We went over to Scotland and did the same venues in Glasgow and then we went down to England and played in The Boston Club, Tufnell Park; The Foresters in Tooting; The Manor House in Manor House – all in London – and The Irish Centre in Leeds. That band stayed together until April 1984.

The support from people outside the business when we were starting off was a huge help. People like Anne Breslin and Ann Birrane, who used to secure dates for us in London. I first met Ann Birrane when I was in Margaret's band. Ann would even send me the fare to come over and do the shows. And the six of us used to stay with Anne Breslin and her husband in Archway Road. It was always people outside showbusiness who gave me support in the early days.

A woman called Nan Moy was managing my sister Margaret when I was a member of her band. Nan and I always got on well together, so when she was parting company with Margaret, we decided we'd start a band together. That turned out to be The Grassroots and we launched it on 15 June 1984.

The Grassroots featured Gerard Gallagher, Larry Gallagher, Gerry Flynn, Roy Campbell, Jimmy Hussey and Tommy Shanley. But two days before our first performance, we were having problems getting an official line-up together. In fact, we didn't have a band. So I phoned Jim the Cope, who was organising the dance, to tell him there was no way we could start on the Friday.

Jim revealed that he had already advertised the group and we would have to play.

If he had said he'd cancel it I might never have restarted, because everything seemed to be going wrong at that point. Between the jigs and the reels, we got a band together for the night. I remember being down in Dublin trying to organise it. I was virtually broke. I was staying with my brother James, so I didn't have the expense of accommodation. But on one of the days I was out around the city and I was faced with the choice of having a Big Mac and chips in McDonald's and walking home, or just having chips and getting the bus home. I was totally addicted to McDonald's at the time, so I ended up walking home.

The band I eventually rustled up for the night was like James Last's, it was so big, except that one half didn't know what the other half was doing. There must have been about seven in the group, when there should only have been four. But I suppose there was safety in numbers. We got through the night and there was a good crowd at the venue.

Then we went down to Kerry the next night and there was nobody in the place. That was a regular experience in the early days. There would often be more people on the stage than on the dancefloor. But I never 'died' on stage, meaning I always played to the best of my ability even when hardly anybody had turned up to see me. It didn't knock my confidence as a performer and I had the attitude that 'the show must go on'.

I recall playing down in Julian's of Midfield, County Mayo, one night and there were only a half-dozen people there. I put on a great show, even if I do say so myself. And John Julian said to me later, 'Do you know, if you don't succeed there's no justice.' I never forgot those words.

Like every band, I had my share of good and bad experiences on the road during those early days. There were lots of long journeys in the back of a van. And the most bizarre incident happened on a trip from England to Scotland. At the time, I had a van that I bought in Dublin, which ran on petrol and gas. During the journey there was a big bang and I thought the gas was blowing up. We stopped and jumped out of the wagon, but everything seemed to be okay. We continued on down the road and the van started heating up. There was no water in it. They all looked at me.

'What are you going to do?'

'What am *I* going to do?'

And me knowing nothing about vans and engines.

We had no water. It was pouring out of the heavens. We were on the motorway. We'd go a bit. We'd stop. The van would cool down. Off we'd go again. It would heat up again.

So, I called on the boyo up above, St Anthony, a man I always had great faith in. I said: 'Now, me boy, this is a crucial point. It's now or never to prove yourself to me.'

Soon after that we approached roadworks and in the distance I could see a hut. I told the driver to pull up and we got out. It was a workman's hut and the big padlock was open and hanging on the door. We went in and there in the middle of that hut was a big five-gallon jar of water!

That was a miracle to me because it was exactly what I needed at that time. It's an experience I'll never forget. I suppose St Anthony knew he was history with me if he didn't come up trumps that time.

There were times when the six of us had to sleep in the back of the van. On another occasion, the whole lot of us stayed in what they called a family room in a service station. It cost £24 for the gang of us and I said to the woman, 'Does it matter if we don't have a mother with us?'

There were lots of long journeys in those days. I always found the trips from Manchester to London and Belmullet to Dublin the most exhausting. But I never really hated the travelling because I always knew there was something good at the end of it. THE STAGE.

Nan Moy was more than just a manager. She was also a good friend. And she tried extra hard, with sometimes very little result. We were surviving, but only just.

I remember one night I had spent hours in a car travelling hundreds of miles to a venue outside Charleville, County Cork, and I got there to find only a handful of people at the dance. It was a big, long dancehall and I could see my friend Josephine down at the door collecting the cash because there were so few in the place. On the way back, we spent the money in a Kentucky Fried Chicken take-away. That was typical of how it was in those days. We did, in turn, perform in places like The Gresham and The National ballrooms in London and stuffed them. From 1984 into 1985 we were doing a roaring trade in big venues around England, but nothing was happening for us in Ireland.

In 1985, I performed at the Irish Festival in London. I had also performed there in 1982 with Margaret, and I remember thinking on that occasion, 'I'd love to top the bill here some day.' Ten years later my dream came true. And my performance there in 1985 was instrumental in getting me noticed by the 'right' people. Not that I was aware of it.

For some time, a man called Bill Delaney of I and B Records in England had been telling Ritz Records boss Mick Clerkin about 'this fella called Daniel O'Donnell who is causing a ripple'. And I remember somebody saying to me at that time: 'You should be with Mick Clerkin. Ritz is the company for you.'

Ritz had already done great things for Foster and Allen and The Fureys, giving them pop chart success. Both acts even appeared on *Top of the Pops*, which had a huge impact at the time. I knew that Mick Clerkin would be a tremendous asset to have behind me, but my feeling was 'Sure why would he be bothered with me?'

But fortune smiled upon me, and when I did the Irish Festival in 1985, Mick was there. It turned out to be one of my best performances. I got a great reaction. Mick saw it and he later contacted me. He offered me the chance to record an album with Ritz and the result was *Two Sides of Daniel O'Donnell*, which was released in the autumn of 1985.

Prior to that I had already recorded an album, *The Boy from Donegal*. It featured 'My Donegal Shore', 'The Old Rustic Bridge', 'Galway Bay', 'Forty Shades of Green', 'My Side of the Road', '5,000 Miles from Sligo', 'The Old Bog Road', 'Slievenamon', 'Noreen Bawn', 'Ballyhoe', 'Home Is Where the Heart Is' and 'Shutters and Boards'.

Nan Moy was still my manager at that time. But I knew that Nan and I were never going to make it together. We had already spent a lot of money and we might as well have been flushing it down a loo, because we were never going to get it back the way we were going.

At this point, I was faced with probably one of the hardest decisions I've ever had to make in my life. On Friday, 13 December 1985 – and I'm superstitious – I remember stopping in Ballisodare, County Sligo, on the way to a venue and phoning Mick Clerkin for an appointment. I had decided to part company with Nan Moy. And I was hoping to persuade Ritz to take over total control of my career.

I had made my decision in Manchester at the beginning of December. Coming out of the Ardree Club, I said to Loretta Flynn, who was then my Fan Club secretary and personal assistant, 'This isn't working.' The thought of giving it all up and doing something else even crossed my mind. I didn't realise that the record 'My Donegal Shore' was then getting a lot of airplay and gaining momentum. I didn't realise that the local radio stations were picking up on it.

I went to see Mick Clerkin and, to my amazement, he was interested in me. He didn't know what arrangement I had with Nan, and whether or not I would part company with her. But I knew then what I had to do. I told Nan that it wasn't working, that Ritz were interested in me and that I was leaving her. It was a dreadful decision to have to make.

At the time, Nan was naturally upset over it and it took her a little time to accept it. It definitely put a strain on our friendship, but only for a short time. Nan knows now, as she did shortly afterwards, that it was for the best. And we are still great friends. She is very much a part of my life and I'm delighted with that, because in our day we had some great times on the road while we struggled to overcome the seemingly endless obstacles that we encountered.

Today, we can look back and laugh at some of the experiences we had. Like the day she phoned me to tell me that the van had been lifted [repossessed] because we couldn't make the repayments. It was the day before one of our shows in Manchester.

'Sure we can hire another van for the show,' I said, unperturbed by this latest catastrophe to befall the band.

But there was even worse news. 'The gear was in the van and that's been lifted too,' she replied.

Now THAT was a problem. But you become very enterprising when you're in a struggling band and living hand-to-mouth. My accordion player, Ronnie Kennedy, and I decided to go over on the plane and link up with some of the musicians in the resident band there. So we headed off with only an accordion and a string machine. We were like Laurel and Hardy. But we got by on the night, playing with the resident group in Manchester.

Then we had to go on to Newcastle, where we teamed up with a guitarist and a drummer for the show. The only song in the whole repertoire that the guitar player knew was 'It's a Long Way to Tipperary'. I don't know how we did it, but we managed to get through that night too. We told the people in both venues that the reason we couldn't bring over our full band was that the back axle had fallen off the van. We couldn't tell them the real story. Mind you, the back axle had previously fallen off, so we weren't telling a lie; we were just stretching the truth a little!

Then there was the time that Nan and I went down to Dublin to pick up the first ever colour posters that we had printed for advertising our shows. I suppose that was a big day in my career then. My own colour posters. On the way back through Donegal, we got a puncture on the Gweebarra bends, a stretch of road between Maas and Leiter. It was dark. It was wet. It was windy. At the time, I hadn't a clue how to change a wheel. Even to this day, changing a wheel is still a major ordeal for me. I opened the boot of the car and a whole load of the posters blew away across the fields. Nan had safety nuts on the wheel and I couldn't get them off. It was a nightmare. Those sorts of things happened on a regular basis. But nowadays we can look back on them and fall around the place laughing.

I finished up with Nan and the band in January 1986 and went off the road.

CHAPTER 8

THE TWO SIDES

As the bells rang out on New Year's Eve, heralding the arrival of 1986, and the frenzied celebrations got into full swing, I was quietly pondering the year ahead. I was really snapping at my last bite of the showbiz cherry. If my new association with Ritz didn't work out, then it was the end of the road for me.

I was now twenty-four years old and life was passing me by. By this stage, most of my friends from school were engaged in secure jobs. Some of them were married and had started a family. Their lives were blossoming along the traditional route. But I still had nothing to show for all my hard work. I didn't even have a car. I had no money. Worse than that, I was up to my neck in debt.

As far as I was concerned, I had made absolutely no headway in my drive to establish my name as a singer. My life was really in tatters and it was make-or-break time. But I hadn't contemplated a life away from the stage. I wasn't qualified to do anything else. I couldn't even play a musical instrument. My future certainly looked very bleak indeed if the year ahead didn't bear some fruit. It began to dawn on me that I might have to take the emigrant boat or plane, like a multitude of my fellow countrymen and women, and start a new life in America or far-away Australia.

It was with some trepidation, then, that I began my relationship with Ritz Records and the man behind the successful company, Mick Clerkin. When I look back now, I realise that I had absolutely no concept of the huge network of contacts and expertise that Ritz would employ to launch Daniel O'Donnell. I knew they had been very successful with other artistes. But I suppose I never put it down to the record company; I probably attributed it to the artistes themselves. Foster and Allen, Davey Arthur and The Fureys were already big names when they joined Ritz, so I believed that had something to do with the success they achieved after they joined the company. On the other hand, I was virtually unknown and I hadn't achieved any success worth talking about.

Looking back over my life, it's not easy to select the greatest moments or the best experiences. But a guy called Sean Reilly rates among the best things that ever happened to me in my whole life, without a shadow of doubt. After I left Nan Moy and joined Ritz, I had no one to take personal control of my career. Ritz had taken responsibility for managing me, but it wasn't possible for Mick Clerkin to run his organisation and give me individual attention. It was at that stage that Sean Reilly came into my life.

Sean comes from the same Irish county as Mick Clerkin – they are both Cavan men. And it was Mick who suggested that Sean might be the man for me. He told me that Sean was a professional manager with many years' experience in the business, that he had a great reputation and was highly respected among his peers, and that he was a guy I could work well with. I had no idea then that I was going to meet a prince of a man who has become as important to me as any member of my own family. He's a man I would go on to trust implicitly with my private as well as my business affairs. Today, Sean Reilly is like a brother and a father to me.

I remember meeting Sean in Dublin's Gresham Hotel at the beginning of 1986. I wanted so much to create the right impression that day. I had never met Sean before, but I realised he was the guy who would be rooting for me in my bid for stardom. So, the day I met him, I wanted him to see a guy who had potential if only it was harnessed and steered in the right direction. I wanted him to believe in me because I believed in myself. Even though years of hard graft had yielded virtually nothing, I still knew that I had the makings of a top-level performer.

Sean is a quiet-spoken man who is very down-to-earth. And I knew instantly that we were going to get on well together. I had a letter one time from a fan who is wheelchair-bound and she paid me a lovely compliment by telling me that I look at her and see a person in a chair, rather than a chair with a person in it. I soon discovered that it's the same with Sean. He sees a person who sings, rather than a singer who is a person.

During that meeting, I knew instinctively that he was a man I could trust with my life, as, indeed, I have done. He exudes an understated confidence. I left the hotel that day with a happy heart and a great weight lifted from my shoulders. My life was beginning to come together again.

Mick Clerkin is a man of few words. He doesn't believe in a lot of small talk. He doesn't give you the type of salesman spiel you get from a lot of guys in this business. His conversation is not peppered with a load of hype. Mick is also down-to-earth – it must be something to do with the laid-back lifestyle around picturesque County Cavan. So, I now had two good men backing me.

At the time, however, I didn't realise how much time, effort and financial resources were going to be invested in Daniel O'Donnell. I had absolutely nothing myself. I was still stone broke, not a penny to my name. It was Mick Clerkin who put all the money behind me initially. Of course, he obviously recognised the potential. But nothing is a sure-fire winner, especially in this business. Thank God he had the courage to go with his gut instinct. A lot of others didn't give me any chance whatsoever.

There's hardly a band manager in Ireland who wasn't approached to take me on in the early stages before Ritz. And they all turned me down! I'll never forget one guy's words. He told me, 'Ah, you'll last about six months.' I suppose they all thought that the type of songs I was singing were out-dated, out of fashion and that I was out of my mind if I thought I was ever going to get anywhere with them. Mick Clerkin took a different view and obviously had more foresight. He took a chance on me. And, of course, it's a two-way thing. An empty bag will never look full, no matter what you do with it. I was somebody Ritz could do something with.

I remember hearing about one Irish newspaper article which referred to me as the 'designer bogman'. It was a put-down line, something I had experienced quite a lot from the trendy types in the media in Ireland at that time. I suppose the insinuation was that I was a brainless mannequin who had been styled and dressed up, then programmed to sing the type of songs in my repertoire.

Nothing could be further from the truth.

It wasn't like that at all with Ritz. There was no physical grooming involved. They didn't try to alter my stage act in any way. Granted, professional photography was employed for my promotional material. But that's a feature of the business that every artiste or group utilises. They did buy me a new wardrobe, simply because I didn't have a great variety of stage gear. I realise that my hair always looks so perfect – not a hair out of place – but that's just the way it is naturally. I don't have to do an awful lot with it. When I go out on stage, it probably looks as if I've spent several hours brushing it. In fact, after I wash and dry it, I just have to run my fingers through it and it's fine.

Back then, I wasn't a fan of having my photo taken and I recall being very nervous doing my first studio shoot for the album cover of *Two Sides of Daniel O'Donnell* in 1985. The man who Ritz employed to set up and direct that shoot was Mick McDonagh, who would work with me on photo shoots and video recordings over the decades that followed.

A friend, Ann O'Connor, cut my hair for those first pictures. And I brought along some of my own clothes, including a suit, a pair of khaki trousers and a short-sleeved white top, with string netting on the chest and sleeves.

The photographer was a lady called Ursula Steiger, as Mick felt it would be less intimidating for me working with a female. The only problem was that Ursula spoke English with what sounded like a German accent. It made her requests seem like very stern demands: 'You will smile! You must smile!', she'd say. I just wanted to cry!

I felt so uncomfortable during that shoot, which was no fault of Ursula's. It's just that back then I didn't know how to stand or pose. Some people said I looked broody in the pictures from that studio session, but

I wouldn't have known what broody was. It was just me not knowing whether to laugh or cry at the time.

***

At this point I needed a band, so Ritz got to work on that as well. Around the time that Ritz took me over, a professional Irish band called Jukebox were splitting up, so Ritz signed them up to be my backing band.

Jukebox consisted of Billy Burgoyne, Tony Murray and Pearse Dunne. And I brought Ronnie Kennedy with me. Ronnie and I related so well together. We had a wonderful understanding. I think everybody could see that on stage. Sometimes you meet a person and you know that you're going to get on so well together. You also know that he or she is going to be the first person you're going to have a row with. That's the sign of a good friendship. Because someone you never have a row with, you never really have a friendship with either. I realise that now. With Ronnie, I knew there were going to be lots of rows and that we'd get on like brothers.

From the moment I started on the road as part of the Ritz enterprise, I never had a bad night. Our first show was on 6 March 1986, in St Cyprian's Club in Brockley, Kent. There was a good turnout, it was a good show and from there a tornado just swept me along and took me to heights beyond my greatest expectations.

For me, the period from January to March 1986 was like getting up in the morning in daylight having gone to bed in the dark. The first couple of months of that year were my dark period. It was a period of uncertainty. But once I got on the road, a whole new world was beginning to open up for me.

If any struggling young performer came up to me today and asked me what is the secret ingredient of my success, I still could not put my finger on it. Why did it all suddenly happen for me overnight after I joined up with Ritz? I suppose it was a combination of having a good band and a professional machine behind me. Ritz pulled out all the stops to ensure that everybody knew about me and that I got maximum exposure. I was their 'priority' act and they pumped everything into 'breaking' me.

One unusual feature of the Irish scene at that time which worked to my advantage was the plethora of pirate radio stations that had captured the imagination of the nation, particularly around rural Ireland. The national music station was then Radio 2. It was primarily a pop and rock station. Up-and-coming singers like myself who were turning out the country and Irish songs didn't get a look in. Disco music had seen to that. It killed off a lot of the live bands in Ireland, and the country's once thriving ballrooms were being deserted for the trendy clubs with flashing lights and loud music.

From the heady days of the sixties – when a big showband star, the late Larry Cunningham, is often quoted as having remarked, 'I haven't seen floorboards since Christmas' – the ballroom crowds had dwindled to such an extent that there wasn't a dancing foot to raise the dust. Rural ballrooms that once almost burst at the joints because of overcrowding were now sad, empty shells in the middle of nowhere. And where once upon a time Joe Dolan could be heard belting out 'The Westmeath Bachelor' or 'Tar and Cement', only the sound of the wind whistling in the bushes broke the night silence.

I'm not blaming Radio 2 in Ireland for the demise of that scene. It was just changing trends and fashion. And they had to go with the music of the day to capture the young listeners.

I do think, however, that they underestimated the sizeable support that still existed for the type of music that myself and tens of thousands of other people have taken to our hearts. There was still a major following for country music and Irish songs, and that soon emerged when the pirate radio stations started mushrooming around Ireland.

Suddenly, artistes like myself had access to the airwaves again. Whereas on Radio 2 you might be lucky to get a few plays for your record, the pirates would play it several times a day. And that helped to bring Irish artistes to the fore again. It turned them into stars all over again.

And I do believe that it rejuvenated the live venues, as the disco clubs began to lose their gloss. Radio 2 in Ireland, now known as 2FM, later changed its policy for a while and introduced two weekend shows featuring country and Irish music, which were presented by Alan Corcoran. And during the week, daily shows also played music by artistes like myself. Sadly, that didn't last and Irish music artistes are still fighting for airtime.

So, back then I happened to come along at the right time in Ireland. The disco scene had peaked and the pirate radio stations captured a growing market all around the country for what artists like myself had to offer. They were playing Big Tom. They were playing Philomena Begley. They were playing Margo. Artistes that were already household names.

And when they started to play Daniel O'Donnell, people began to sit up and take notice. I was a new name. A new voice. An unknown quantity. There was a curiosity value attached to Daniel O'Donnell. Who is he? Where has he suddenly come from? And I was the first of a new breed of singers to emerge.

I'm glad that the right set of circumstances came along at that time to give me lift-off. I do believe that if you persevere for long enough you will eventually get the rewards you're seeking. Nothing comes easy in this life. You have to get out there and fight for it.

The pirate radio stations right across Ireland picked up on *Two Sides of Daniel O'Donnell*. That album featured 'The Green Glens of Antrim', 'The Blue Hills of Breffni', 'Any Tipperary Town', 'The Latchyco', 'Home Town on the Foyle', 'These Are My Mountains', 'My Donegal Shore', 'Crying My Heart Out Over You', 'My Old Pal', 'Our House Is a Home', 'Your Old Love Letters', '21 Years', 'Highway 40 Blues' and 'I Wouldn't Change You If I Could', all of which were capturing the attention of radio listeners.

Meanwhile, the band was taking a while to settle down, as new bands do. John Staunton joined in the summer of 1986. Billy Condon joined in the summer of 1987. Kevin Sheerin and John Ryan joined in the spring of 1988, and that line-up remained intact until I was forced to go off the road at the beginning of 1992, of which more later. When I resumed my stage performing after a break of four months, Kevin and John didn't return. They had decided to pursue other projects. It was an amicable parting and they were replaced in my band by Richard Nelson and Raymond McLoughlin.

Every night at the end of a performance, I take time out to introduce the individual members of my group to the audience. And I always tell the people who come to see us that to me they are the best band in the world. I tell them that I have tremendous admiration for all the lads. And that's not just throwaway spiel. Perhaps when you say something like that at the end of each show it becomes meaningless. But my tribute to the lads is quite sincere. I really do mean what I say. My show would be nothing without the contribution from the musicians who have worked with me. It's not just me out there on stage doing all the work. Without a good band behind me it would be a totally different show.

Although we started off attracting big crowds, we weren't playing to full houses immediately. But it wasn't long before the queues started to form outside venues around Ireland. This was a new phenomenon. It was reminiscent of the old Irish showband days back in the 'swinging sixties' when the ballrooms were in full flight, struggling to cope with the crowds that created the sweaty atmosphere.

I believe that once the 'bush telegraph' started spreading the word that this new guy Daniel O'Donnell was something of a sensation, it had a knock-on effect. I was now a curiosity item and more and more people started coming out to see what all the fuss was about. Maybe initially they came along for that reason, but I was obviously doing something right because they kept on coming back again and again and again.

I don't think I was aware of the full extent of my drawing power at that time. I didn't dwell on it. I was just happy to see lots of people at my shows. And there were thousands of people coming to see us. People kept telling me, 'It's like the old showband days.' I wasn't thinking along those lines because I was never a part of the old ballroom days. I had heard about it. I had read about it. But it was before my time. And I wasn't conscious of the fact that I was creating a whole new dancing scene in Ireland. I didn't realise that I was introducing a new generation to the joy of dancing to the sound of a live band on stage.

I think the first time I consciously started to notice the crowds was in 1986 when we performed in Dungiven in the north of Ireland. The band arrived at the venue at seven o'clock in the evening to set up their gear and there was a queue of people already waiting in line outside the building. When I heard that I thought it was quite incredible, because our show didn't start until eleven o'clock that night!

In the early stages, I was much more popular in the North and was attracting bigger crowds there. But I soon began to see the same trend developing in the Republic. The first time I noticed it there was when we played in Enniskean, County Cork. This was our second visit. We had had a reasonably large crowd the first time, but upon our return it was packed. That soon became the norm right across the country.

Two Sides of Daniel O'Donnell established me as a recording artiste. It brought me a long way in Ireland and got people familiar with the type of material that is now my trademark. But it was the follow-up album, *I Need You*, that helped to launch my career in Britain.

I Need You was also my first scary experience of making a video, which included a screen kiss!

CHAPTER 9

I NEED YOU

Throughout my years in showbiz, I have encountered some really bizarre coincidences and experiences. And one of them involved the song 'I Need You'.

One night we were playing in a venue called The Georgian, in Ballina, County Mayo, and a fan called Anne, whom I had known for some time, came up to me. She started talking about this song from the sixties that her sister liked and she suggested that it would be my type of song. So, I asked her to send it on to me. One day it arrived in the post. She had recorded it on to a tape, obviously from an old record because it was quite noisy and crackly.

The moment I played it I knew that it did suit me and I loved it. 'I Need You' had been a big hit in Ireland in 1965 for Declan Ryan and The Regal Showband from Cork. Written by American songwriter Baker Knight, whose song 'The Wonder of You' was a smash hit for Elvis Presley, 'I Need You' has also enjoyed chart success in the States for US singer Rick Nelson.

The strange thing about that song is, when I took it down to Ritz in Dublin to suggest recording it, Mick Clerkin already had it in his possession. He had picked it up from a totally different source during the same period and he was going to suggest it to me as a suitable song!

I still find that very strange. It's as if some supernatural force had a hand in it.

I recorded the album *I Need You* towards the end of 1986, and in addition to the title track, it featured 'Sing an Old Irish Song', 'From a Jack to a King', 'Lovely Rose of Clare', 'Stand Beside Me', 'Irish Eyes', 'Dear Old Galway Town', 'Three Leaf Shamrock', 'Veil of White Lace', 'Kickin' Each Other's Hearts Around', 'Medals for Mothers', 'Wedding Bells', 'Snowflakes', 'Your Friendly Irish Way', 'Lough Melvin's Rocky Shore' and 'I Love You Because'. When Ritz started promoting that album in Britain, the reaction to it was very favourable and it started to move.

In the days when a lot of the old songs were written, there was no such thing as a video. But when I started out in my career the video had certainly made a huge impact on the music industry. In the pop world it was the video that could often make the song a hit.

So I had to make a video, whether I liked it or not. And I certainly wasn't jumping up and down with glee about doing it. Mick McDonagh was back to guide me through it, so off I went into this strange new world. This part of the music industry is something that never crossed my mind when I decided that I wanted to be a professional singer. If I wanted to be in the movies I would have become an actor.

The video was shot in a few locations around Dublin, including Herbert

Park in Ballsbridge and Grafton Street. In one scene I'm lost in love, peering out of the window of a house on a leafy road. Eventually I meet the girl who has captured my heart. She was a lovely blonde young woman called Debbie Bowes, who had been hired for the video. We have a romantic dinner and then at the end of the evening I pop the question. I remember getting the ring out and trying to smile as I clumsily put it on her finger.

Then the dreadful moment arrived when I had to do my first – and last – kiss. When I think back on that today I laugh out loud at how young and innocent and naïve I was at the time. I remember being afraid to be too enthusiastic about the kiss in case Debbie might think I was doing it for real. I was horribly shy and was glad when it was all over.

The next evening I picked up the *Evening Herald* newspaper and spotted my video fiancée modeling underwear. God only knows what she thought of me!

***

I continued touring and playing to new audiences. In the spring of 1987, I went to Inverness, Scotland, to perform in The Eden Court theatre for the first time. For some reason, I always wanted to sing in the north of Scotland. I remember seeing Inverness in a tour brochure of Irish country singer Susan McCann, and I instantly became attracted to it. So Inverness was always on my mind as a place to perform, and going there was the realisation of yet another dream.

Now Inverness is very special to me because it was there that I got my first ever standing ovation. It took me completely by surprise when the audience stood up at the end and clapped for several minutes. It was something I had never experienced before. And I didn't know how to respond to it. I remember thinking, 'I should be doing something special now to justify this.' But apart from a somersault, there was nothing more I could do.

The Theatre Royal in Norwich, England, is another venue that will always be special to me. It was in Norwich that I performed to a predominantly English audience for the first time. I'll never forget that night. I was so nervous. I suppose it was fear of the unknown. I had performed in England many times before that, but this was different. On the previous trips over, I had played Irish venues with an Irish audience, and I was fairly relaxed because I was confident that they would be familiar with the songs. Norwich was going to be a different scene altogether.

When I arrived at the venue, my first question to the promoter, Dick Condon, was, 'Will there be many Irish people at the show?' And the reply I got was, 'About 10 per cent.'

My heart sank into my stomach. Oh, holy God, I thought, how am I going to survive the night at all? I went out to the wings that night to see the 'warm up' band perform – they were English – and my reaction was, 'I'll never be as good as that!'

But eventually my turn arrived and I started into my show. Once I found myself on stage I was fine. And, to my surprise, the audience gave me an enthusiastic response and took me to their hearts. I realised then that there was more to Irish music: that it didn't just appeal to Irish people.

Before I went to Norwich, I hadn't even heard of the place. I didn't know it existed. Years later, I told the audience there that way back then I thought Norwich was a building society!

'I Need You' is the song that the people in Inverness and Norwich were familiar with. It opened the swinging doors for me across Britain.

Thanks, Anne!

I have done many concert tours covering Scotland, England and Wales, and I'm always well received. The enthusiasm of the audience has never diminished. It remains a mystery to me. My repertoire doesn't alter to any great extent, yet the people who come to my shows still greet every song with the same degree of affection. Perhaps they regard the songs as old friends? But words can't adequately describe how I feel about the reception I receive on my tours.

In 1987, I recorded the album *Don't Forget to Remember*, which, in addition to the title track, featured the songs 'I Don't Care', 'Old Loves Never Die', 'I Wonder Where You Are Tonight', 'Don't Be Angry', 'Roses Are Red', 'Before I'm Over You', 'Take Good Care of Her', 'Pretty Little Girl from Omagh', 'Green Willow', 'Don't Let Me Cross Over', 'The Good Old Days', 'Pat Murphy's Meadow' and 'I Just Can't Make It on My Own'.

It was also the year that I did my first major festival in Britain.

In the early stages, festivals were a challenge to me. And I wanted to do them. The Peterborough festival was where I made my country music debut in 1987. And it was a huge success for me. It drew attention to me as a performer because of all the publicity surrounding that extravaganza, and it helped to get me noticed by an even wider audience.

In October 1987, following Peterborough, I embarked on my first major nationwide UK tour. It was another milestone in my career – performing the concert circuit.

While I was apprehensive starting out, I soon relaxed when I saw the response and out of the twenty-two dates, sixteen were sell-out shows. My career had now moved into top gear and I was performing in a new league. The sun was really shining on my world. This was what I had always worked

towards. Yet when it happened it seemed too good to be true. It was difficult for me to comprehend how far I had progressed since joining Ritz. I
felt it was better not to dwell on it and I just put my head down and kept
on working flat out.

When you're struggling, nothing seems to go right. But when you get
rolling, everything fits into place. When I was in Inverness, Eamon Leahy,
my then tour director who had also played a big role in getting my career
on the road, came into my dressing room and told me that the *I Need You*
album was going into the British Country Chart at No. 14.

At that time, I wasn't even aware that there was a British Country Chart.
Wasn't I very naive? My heart skipped a beat with excitement and I went
scouring magazines to find the chart. The album went into the Top 10 the
following week, 28 March 1987.

Three months later, my earlier album *Two Sides of Daniel O'Donnell*
made its chart entry. And at the end of August 1987, 'Take Good Care
of Her'/'Summertime in Ireland' made it to the No. 1 spot in the Irish
singles charts.

That was one of the most exciting experiences of my life. My first No. 1.

The Irish charts show, then presented by Larry Gogan on Radio 2, was
broadcast every Sunday. Ritz had had an indication that the song had
gone into the No. 1 position, but I still tuned in to hear the charts that
weekend and I was thrilled when Larry announced, 'At number one it's
Daniel O'Donnell and "Take Good Care of Her".' My heart was pound-
ing. I was totally elated. It was wonderful.

I don't get much satisfaction out of making records – it's something that
I have to do and I do it to the best of my ability. But I don't actually enjoy
the recording process because there is no audience there to lift you and to

bounce off. I miss that. The only fun I get out of making records is watching them perform in the charts. I love the charts. And getting a No. 1 still gives me a kick. The week I had my first No. 1 coincided with my holidays. But I remember how I wanted to go back to work and sing all that week.

On 31 October, within one week of its release, *Don't Forget to Remember* entered the UK Country Chart at No. 1. That achievement certainly took my breath away. I could scarcely believe it. It was like having a fairy god-mother wave a magic wand and make all the things that I wished happen for me. I think it took Ritz completely by surprise, as it did everyone else, because this had all happened in less than two years.

My next album, *From the Heart*, repeated that achievement on 29 October 1988. It's a fifties and sixties album, featuring 'The Minute You're Gone', 'It Doesn't Matter Anymore', 'Mary from Dungloe', 'Bye Bye Love', 'The Old Rugged Cross', 'Wasting My Time', 'Kelly', 'Things', 'Act Naturally', 'Honey', 'Wooden Heart', 'It Keeps Right on a-Hurting', 'My Bonnie Maureen', 'I Know That You Know', 'Old Dungarvan Oak' and 'Danny Boy'. *From the Heart* also crossed over into the British pop charts, where it remained for twelve weeks. I'd say that had U2 worried for a while!

The year 1988 marked another landmark in my career when I performed at the Wembley Country Music Festival. That was always a big event, attracting the legendary country music stars from America.

My first trip to Wembley was in 1979, when I went over to see Kitty Wells. Kitty was the first female country singer in America to sell a million records, with her hit 'It Wasn't God Who Made Honky Tonk Angels'. That visit to the Wembley festival was a real thrill. It was thronged with people and there was a great atmosphere. I didn't imagine then that one day I would be sharing that same limelight. It was a great sensation.

I also made my Nashville debut in 1988, when I represented Ireland at Fan Fair, the showcase for international country music artistes. I sang 'Take Good Care of Her', 'Don't Let Me Cross Over' and 'Don't Be Angry' before an audience of fifteen thousand, and I was very happy with the reaction. The backing group was the legendary Jordanaires, who had performed with 'The King', Elvis Presley. But the most exciting aspect of that trip was my performance at Nashville's famous Grand Ole Opry, as guest of George Hamilton IV, who, sadly, has since passed on. The country boy from Donegal on stage at the Grand Ole Opry! It was hard to take it all in.

The following day, I took the stage at Summer Lights, Nashville's annual four-day street festival, with concert platforms erected in six downtown locations and many of country music's top entertainers performing. I appeared on an open stage outside the Nashville Courthouse – I mustn't have murdered the country songs because they didn't lock me up! – and I shared the bill with George Hamilton IV, Lorrie Morgan and Ricky Skaggs, which was a great honour.

A couple of nights later, I was invited to appear at the prestigious Stock-yards nightspot by the owner, music publishing magnate Buddy Killen, and I got a very enthusiastic response to my four-song set.

We returned to Nashville six months later and I was invited to perform on the famous *Nashville Now* TV show, which was televised throughout the United States and Canada and hosted by Ralph Emery. It was during this visit that I began working with top record producer Allen Reynolds, who had been responsible for hits by such artistes as Don Williams, Crystal Gayle, Kathy Mattea and Garth Brooks.

From our very first meeting I knew I was going to get on well with Allen. Work on my Nashville album *The Last Waltz* got under way, but in the meantime I released two new albums, *Thoughts of Home* and *Favourites*, which also headed straight for that top spot in Britain.

Thoughts of Home had 'My Shoes Keep Walking Back to You', 'Mountains of Mourne', 'London Leaves', 'Blue Eyes Crying in the Rain', 'Old Days Remembered', 'Send Me the Pillow You Dream On', 'Moonlight and Roses', 'A Little Piece of Heaven', 'Far Far from Home', 'Isle of Innisfree', 'My Heart Skips a Beat', 'I Know One', 'I'll Take You Home Again Kathleen', 'Second Fiddle', 'My Favourite Memory' and 'Forty Shades of Green'.

Favourites featured 'Bed of Roses', 'Forever You'll Be Mine', 'Excuse Me (I Think I've Got a Heartache)', 'Halo of Gold', 'The Streets of Baltimore', 'Geisha Girl', 'Life to Go', 'That's a Sad Affair', 'Bringing Mary Home', 'Home Sweet Home', 'The Banks of My Own Lovely Lee', 'Home Is Where the Heart Is', 'Dublin in the Rare Ould Times' and 'The Green Hills of Sligo'.

Both albums also entered the pop charts, and *Thoughts of Home* was named as Britain's 1989 Country Album of the Year at the Music Week Awards, the UK's weekly music industry publication.

I was very apprehensive about going to Nashville to work. An Irish guy going over to record country songs in the home of country! It was a bit like taking snow to Alaska. I had already met Allen Reynolds and I felt comfortable with him, but I didn't know what people would expect of me. I didn't know what they were going to think of me. How are they going to react to somebody coming from Ireland and singing country music in the way that I do? But I wasn't long in their presence till I felt at home.

The people in Nashville are very warm and embracing. It turned out to be a really good period for me. I wasn't known there and I enjoyed the freedom that that gave me. I enjoyed the quietness. I suppose it gave me time to reflect to some extent on the whirlwind that had propelled me through my career since joining Ritz.

It was a real honour working with a producer of Allen Reynolds' calibre. Over the years he continued to create some of the most successful records to come out of the Nashville studios and, of course, he was one of the people behind the phenomenal success of country superstar Garth Brooks.

The title for the *Last Waltz* album is derived from the very popular song included on it, 'Last Waltz of the Evening', which was written by an Irish-based American, Tom Pacheco. When I heard it first, it didn't really connect with me. But I knew almost immediately that it was for me when I started to sing it.

I feel I made a reasonably good impression in Nashville during my visit. Allen Reynolds was certainly on my side from then on. He made some very complimentary remarks about me on a late-night 2FM radio show in Ireland, hosted by the Irish showbiz chaplain, Fr Brian D'Arcy, who is also a journalist and broadcaster and was one of the first people to give me media exposure in the *Sunday World*, one of Ireland's largest-selling national newspapers, when I was starting out.

Allen did a phone link-up with Fr Brian from Nashville and told the listeners that he liked my singing style and he described it as a 'clean, open singing style'. He said he respected me as a performer and he was impressed by my sense of songs, my commitment to the audience and my joy in performing. Allen told Fr Brian that he always felt there was a common link between Irish music and country music.

When *The Last Waltz* eventually came out, it repeated the success of my other albums, going straight to No. 1 in Britain's country chart as well as entering the pop chart. *The Last Waltz* featured 'Here I Am in Love Again',

'We Could', 'Last Waltz of the Evening', 'When Only the Sky Was Blue', 'Heaven With You', 'You Know I Still Love You', 'Talk Back Trembling Lips', 'The Shelter of Your Eyes', 'When We Get Together', 'Ring of Gold', 'A Fool Such as I', 'Memory Number One', 'Look Both Ways', 'Little Patch of Blue' and 'Marianne'.

In 1991, *The Last Waltz* was voted top album by the British country music magazine *Country Music People*, who also voted me top male vocalist. And Britain's *Country Music Round Up* voted me most popular male vocalist that year.

Another award that I treasure is the one I received in 1989 when I was voted Ireland's Entertainer of the Year. It's always a great honour and a great thrill to receive that kind of recognition in your own country.

***

In 1991 I unwittingly became embroiled in a controversy after I was dropped from the UK Country Chart when the chart's supervisory committee decided to redefine country music and ruled that I wasn't 'pure' country. Six of my albums were dropped, because they were considered 'easy listening' rather than country.

Well, there was an almighty hullabaloo over that decision. I never realised my fans could be so outspoken. (Incidentally, 'fans' is not a term I like, but I suppose there's no other word to describe them.) They bombarded the British Country Music Association with letters of protest. And I was also really chuffed by the fact that all the regional radio stations in Britain supported me in a vigorous fashion and voiced their outrage over the move.

The furore over the charts raged for weeks and made the headlines in newspapers at home and abroad. It was also discussed on radio and television. I was a little embarrassed by all the fuss. They say that there's no such thing as bad publicity, but in the end it was all getting a bit too much. And when the Country Music Association finally reviewed the situation and decided after four months to reverse its decision, I was more than relieved.

I don't know what effect it would have had on my career in the long term if I hadn't been allowed back into the country chart. But it definitely didn't do me any damage during the short period that it lasted. If anything, it increased my profile and probably helped to win me a lot more support. I'm very grateful to the fans, the media and everyone who supported me during that saga.

I suppose it is hard to define the type of music that I do. But I do believe it leans more to country than anything else. I know that many of the songs are middle-of-the-road too. I never record material on the basis that it might be a commercial success for me. That's not the way I operate. And while Ritz might have come up with songs that they would select as a possible chart hit, they never, ever put pressure on me to record anything I didn't want to do. My only rule of thumb is that I will only record a song that I like. So, I suppose all my albums are my own personal favourites.

Songs come to me through different channels. I have already described how I picked up 'I Need You' from a fan.

It was Mick Clerkin who found my second No. 1 hit record, 'My Shoes Keep Walking Back to You'. He heard it one night when he was in Nashville. The flip side of that record was 'Far Far from Home', which was written by a County Cavan man, Hugh Donoghue. Irish songwriters in general have been very good for me. I like Hugh's material. He also wrote 'Eileen', which is on the *Best Of* album. His songs suit me.

Mary Sheridan was another Irish songwriter whose material I liked, and one of her songs, 'Letter from the Postman's Bag', was also included on the *Best Of* album. I was also a fan of the work of John Farry from County Fermanagh. He wrote 'Summertime in Ireland', which was on the flip side of my first Irish No. 1 hit. And he's the songwriter who penned 'Lough Melvin's Rocky Shore' (*I Need You* album). John would later team up with a young man called Nathan Carter as his manager and songwriter.

Songwriters send me material all the time and I do listen to it. Sometimes I find a real gem. All through my career people have suggested songs to me. Even the legendary Irish singer and songwriter Christy Moore helped me out in that department. He came back from Australia with a song for me, which was very kind of him. I look at songs in a personal way. I have to like the sound and the way it flows. The majority of the songs that I do are very, very simple. They have a simple story. They don't demand a lot of attention and you don't need a dictionary to understand them.

***

Of the videos that I recorded back then, I was very happy with 'Thoughts of Home'. There was a lot of drama around the shooting of that video, with Mick McDonagh directing operations once again.

I'm a big fan of Vera Lynn, who found fame during the Second World War. In 1940, she hosted her own BBC radio show called *Sincerely Yours*. During the programme she would read out messages from loved ones to their soldier boyfriends, husbands and sons. She became their link with the men fighting abroad. Vera also became famous for songs like 'We'll Meet Again' and 'White Cliffs of Dover'.

A woman called Joan Tobin, with whom I stayed in England, was a fan of Vera Lynn and she knew that I admired her greatly. In 1989, Vera was due to give a performance at London's Festival Hall and, to my surprise, Joan got us two tickets. I was really looking forward to that concert with the excitement of a child counting down to Christmas morning. I had never seen Vera Lynn perform live on stage.

Then came a shock call from Mick to tell me that the video shoot for 'Thoughts of Home' was set to take place on the same day as Vera's concert. The location for the shoot was Aghadoe Heights Hotel near Killarney, County Kerry! I won't repeat what went through my mind, but I didn't tell Mick.

During the shoot, Mick sensed that there was something on my mind.

'What's wrong, Daniel?' he asked.

'I'll tell you what's wrong, Mick,' I replied. 'Vera Lynn's performing in London tonight and I'm going to be in that audience by hook or by crook.'

You will hardly believe this, but once again there was divine intervention. There was a horse in the field where we were shooting and he galloped over to us, kicking over cameras and causing enough damage to force the cancellation of the video shoot.

I was on a flight out of Kerry like a shot ... and that night I took my seat in the London theatre and was in seventh heaven as I enjoyed an unforgettable concert by the great Vera Lynn!

The video that I liked best in those early days was *An Evening with Daniel O'Donnell*, which was recorded during a live show in Dundee, Scotland. I felt that it was really representative of me as a performer.

My videos have sold exceptionally well and they have all entered the Top 20 pop video charts, alongside the likes of Kylie Minogue, Michael

Jackson, U2, Prince and Madonna. In the same bed as Madonna. Isn't that something else!

***

I'm the type of performer who never gets excited about playing particular venues. Venues are not important to me, no matter how prestigious, or how highly regarded by people in the showbiz world. I only ever judge a show by the audience. Because no matter where you perform, it's not worth talking about if you don't have the audience with you.

However, some venues do act as landmarks in my career. The Grand Ole Opry was special, I do admit, purely because of its historical association with country music.

1988 was the year I performed at The Gaiety Theatre in Dublin, and that registered as a big step up the ladder for me in my own country.

The next 'big' venue was the Royal Albert Hall in London. I have no great memory of that night. I can only recall singing 'The Old Dungarvan Oak' and seeing a Chinese family sitting on the left-hand side. That intrigued me. I don't know where they came from. I don't know what they were doing there. And I have never seen them since that night.

Then, of course, there was Carnegie Hall in New York. Now that sounds really grand, doesn't it? But to me, it's a venue that's only as good as its audience. Getting the opportunity to have my name up in lights at Carnegie Hall had a bigger effect on other people than it did on me.

I was delighted, of course, when I learned that I had a show lined up for that venue. But that was six months before I actually played there, so I didn't dwell on it too much. There were a lot of concerts to play before

Carnegie Hall, and my main concern was the next show. I didn't dismiss everything I had lined up for the six months leading up to it and just live for Carnegie. But when D-day eventually arrived, I began to realise that I was heading into something special. On the other hand, there is always the fear that when something is built up so much, is it going to be everything it's cracked up to be?

My date in Carnegie Hall was during a short tour of the States in 1991, and it did turn out to be an extra special night in that magnificent auditorium. I got a bit emotional when I went out onto the stage, for some strange reason.

I recall how I told the audience, 'I never thought I'd get the opportunity to say this: welcome to Carnegie Hall.' Then I went straight into a song because I felt I was going to break down. I never thought I'd see the day when that would happen to me. A flood of emotions hit me.

I think that was a result of seeing a number of people I knew sitting in the front row. Some friends of mine from home, John and Anna Brennan, were in New York on holidays and they had secured tickets for the front row, as had some people that I knew from Liverpool: Rene, Alison and Joe.

I remember asking myself, 'How did I get here?' I think the memories came flooding back from the days when I couldn't get dates in places that I wanted to play back home when I first started out. Carnegie Hall was the sudden realisation of just how far I had come.

Then I looked down and saw all the familiar faces and my reaction was, 'This is a wonderful night for all of us.'

CHAPTER 10

MY TEAM

The Daniel O'Donnell show is by no means a one-man-band. I would never have achieved so much without the back-up of an outstanding team of people.

Showbiz is a breeding ground for the cynical, the opportunistic and the ruthless. But I have been very lucky with the calibre of the people who work with me.

I have always been surrounded by people who are good for me and people I'm happy with, both on and off the stage. If you're not getting on with the people you work with, then you cannot function to the best of your ability.

There is not a single individual in the organisation that I'm not comfortable with.

And that's very important.

The man who made it all happen for me, of course, was Mick Clerkin of Ritz Records. Mick definitely had the Midas touch. His first big success was way back in 1981/1982 with The Fureys. They had a major hit with 'Sweet Sixteen', which sold a quarter of a million copies. After finding the winning formula, Mick's next successful outing in Britain was with Foster and Allen and their hit 'A Bunch of Thyme'.

By that stage, people were beginning to sit up and take notice of Mick Clerkin. Irish artistes suddenly saw him as a stepping-stone to the top of the showbiz scene in Britain.

Mick's own success as a businessman was not achieved overnight. The affable man from Ballyjamesduff, County Cavan, came up the hard way, serving his apprenticeship when he started as road manager with Larry Cunningham and The Mighty Avons in 1966, after they had a hit with 'Tribute to Jim Reeves'.

When Larry Cunningham decided to leave The Mighty Avons, he asked Mick to become his personal manager. Mick was at first reluctant to take on the daunting task, fearing that he wouldn't be able to do it justice. But Larry obviously recognised Mick's potential way back then and persuaded the County Cavan man to launch a new career. His very first venture as a manager was a tour of the States, which was a big success for Larry Cunningham.

Mick told me that his real love was always the record industry. He later cut his teeth in the business in a Dublin-based company called Release Records. Mick always believed that there was a viable market for middle-of-the-road (MOR) music in Britain. It just needed to be developed.

The record company he owned at the time had a massive Irish hit with the song 'One Day at a Time', sung by the popular Irish singer Gloria.

Mick then approached four major record companies in Britain with the single. But after listening to the first verse and chorus, they all said: 'Thank you very much. Not for Britain.' Mick still believed it had potential in Britain, but he had no outlet there at that time.

A couple of months later, the seed was sown for the emergence of Ritz when an American singer, Lena Martell, released 'One Day at a Time' in the UK and it turned out to be the only million-record seller that year.

The opportunity to have a crack at the British MOR market came along with 'Sweet Sixteen', which was a big hit in Ireland for The Fureys. Their manager, Jim Hand, gave Mick the go-ahead to promote it in Britain.

Mick and a partner, the late Peter Dempsey, went over to London and set up their operation in the London Ryan Hotel, after securing a special rate. They worked out of there for three months.

The late Terry Wogan was on the radio in those days and he was a big support. Terry was always a good man for playing Irish releases if the quality was good. He thought 'Sweet Sixteen' was a magical record and played it on air. It was a massive hit and Mick was on his way as a successful record label boss as the head of Ritz.

BBC Radio 2 in Britain, which has a big influence on record sales, began to support Ritz as a label, recognising that it was releasing good-quality records.

Ritz was a small family-run company, and I believe that was one of the secrets of its success. Mick's policy was to keep the number of artistes on his label to a minimum. By doing that, he ensured that each artist – and we were all different – got individual attention and adequate resources.

Ritz also had a concert division, managed by company director Eamon Leahy. They started on that scene with Foster and Allen and went on to promote all my concerts. Ritz had a very good relationship with regional radio stations around Britain, which most promoters would not have had the same contact with.

A gentleman called Paddy McIntyre worked in promotions and had a full-time job keeping in touch with all the British regional radio stations. I don't think I would be at the level I now enjoy in Britain if it wasn't for the backing of the radio stations in those days.

The Ritz company comprised people who believed in what they were doing and were enthusiastic about the artistes they were promoting.

It's a great feeling to have been a part of the success of Ritz Records and to see Mick Clerkin achieve so much. Ritz was eventually sold, and Mick then formed Rosette Records.

***

I have already documented my feelings for Sean Reilly, who was my manager up to 2015, when he retired.

A native of Kilnaleck, County Cavan, Sean started his working life in a number of jobs. He was a barman for a short time. He worked in a furniture factory. And he was a car salesman.

He was always friendly with the band members in Larry Cunningham's group, The Mighty Avons. And he got to know their road manager, Mick Clerkin.

When Mick went into the record company business, Sean joined him in 1968, working as a roadie with a group called Gary Street and the Fairways. He then progressed to managing that band.

For most of his career, Sean was manager to the highly regarded Irish country singer and songwriter Ray Lynam and his group, The Hillbillies.

I would not have achieved the success I enjoy today had it not been for Sean's guidance. Although he is a very humble man, Sean was always a man of vision. He saw the bigger picture for me, particularly in America.

Sean always believed that there was an audience for me in America and he never gave up on that dream, even though there were many times when I was prepared to throw in the towel when we were struggling to sell shows there.

With the help of PBS television, we eventually got our big break and today places like Branson, Missouri are an important part of my annual concert tours.

It was Sean who also teamed me up with my touring partner Mary Duff. Sean spotted Mary in 1987 in a 'Search for a Star' talent competition run by the *Sunday World* newspaper in Ireland. At this point my career was at a stage where I needed a full-time support artist for the shows. Mary is simply a fabulous entertainer; we work well together and the fans love her.

I have always had a great band behind me – musicians like John Staunton, Billy Burgoyne, Ronnie Kennedy, Tony Murray, Billy Condon, Richard Nelson and Raymond McLoughlin. The fans also loved them, and each individual through the years had his own following. It wasn't unusual at shows to see people coming up with gifts for the lads, as well as for myself. Through the years, I've also had some excellent backing singers on my recordings and live shows, including Danny and Janette Sheerin in the early days, and Leon McCrum and Trionagh Allen who still work with me.

The other members of the team in the early days were Loretta Flynn, Jim Rosie and Joe Collum. Loretta was well known to the fans from her time as the secretary of my Fan Club.

I first met Loretta when she started coming to my shows back in 1984/1985, with her sister and cousin. We struck up a friendship and

Loretta, who is a native of Waterford, took over the running of the Fan Club with her sister, Breda, operating out of the Ritz office. It was always more than a working relationship. We were good friends. And occasionally she would travel with me to concerts. She started looking after my stage clothes. Eventually, it reached the point when she was travelling with me all the time and looking after me. As my workload built up, I found that I needed someone to organise my stage clothes on a full-time basis, so Loretta slipped into that role and has been with me through the decades. However, Loretta will be retiring this year (2017).

***

When my career started to grow and grow, people used to say to me, 'Oh, you'll soon have minders.' I would laugh it off. But then Joe Collum from Ballybofey, County Donegal became a minder of sorts. Joe was my driver when I was working and he was always on hand to make sure that everything ran smoothly at meet-and-greets and so on. I don't know what I would have done without Joe for all those years. He always kept a cool head and he was great in his dealings with the fans.

I never had any worries about my safety or the safety of my fans on tours, apart from one particular night in Middlesbrough when there was a bomb scare and the police evacuated the theatre.

We were all herded out on to the street. And as we waited for the all-clear, I mingled with the crowd and got chatting with the fans. One woman told me how she had come to hear me sing her favourite song, 'The Old Rugged Cross'. So I decided to sing it there and then for her on the street in the middle of a major drama.

The police then came along and suggested that it would be safer if we all made our way up to the local park. That's exactly what we all did. And I got up on a park bench and sang another couple of songs.

Then the police turned up again and this time they offered me the use of the loudhailer in their panda car. I took them up on their offer and sang another few songs through their loudhailer!

Thankfully, no bomb was found in the theatre – but by then we had already had the best night.

**

When I did my first concert shows in 1988 at Dublin's Gaiety Theatre, the promoter was Kieran Cavanagh, a talented man with a long history in the Irish music business. In the 1970s, Sligo-born Kieran toured the dance halls of Ireland himself as the bass player with a group called the New Blues.

Later, Kieran formed his own promotion and production company, KCP, and went on to run Irish tours and concerts for some of the world's iconic artists, including James Brown, Van Morrison, Johnny Cash, Kris Kristofferson, Tammy Wynette, Chuck Berry, Trisha Yearwood and Mary Chapin Carpenter.

Kieran would go on to become the promoter for my Irish concerts, taking me all the way to The Point in Dublin back in 1992. I was lucky to make that early connection with Kieran. My main priority is that the people who spend their money coming to my shows are treated well. And they always are with Kieran, who does everything to the highest standard.

In 1995, Kieran received the prestigious CMA Award for 'International Promoter of the Year'. It was presented to him by Tony Conway, the president of the CMA, at a special dinner in the Nashville Convention Centre.

When my manager, Sean Reilly, retired in 2015 I was very fortunate that Kieran agreed to take over that role in my career. Kieran was already part of 'the family', so to speak, so I wasn't dealing with a stranger. It made the transition very easy for me. I am blessed with Kieran, as he is a lovely man just like Sean.

My niece and god-daughter, Trish Swan (nee Doogan), is my PA and tour manager, and she keeps me on the straight and narrow as regards keeping up with my day-to-day stuff. Trish also looks after my social media. I'd be lost without her.

Trish, who is my sister Kathleen's daughter, made her own splash on social media when she married Neil in February 2017. During the wedding ceremony in our little church in Kincasslagh, a group of well-known singers among the invited guests surprised the happy couple in what local priest Fr Pat Ward described as a 'flash mob Catholic style.'

In a scene straight out of the movie *Love Actually*, Derek Ryan, Shawn Cuddy, John McNicholl, Tony Allen of Foster and Allen, Tony Kenny, Fergal Flaherty, Chris O'Donnell, Vicki Kenny, Trionagh Allen, Annette Griffin, Majella and myself stood up one by one in the congregation to sing a line each from the hymn 'How Great Thou Art'. Then we all strolled on to the altar at the end of the hymn, singing in front of the emotional wedding couple.

The event was organised by Patricia's friend, Gavin Boyle. Apart from the singers involved, nobody knew it was going to happen. It was one of those moments where guests didn't know what was happening, but they knew it was special. There was no rehearsal for it, as that would have given it away. Everybody just stood up in their seat and one by one they started to sing. Patricia had organised everything else to a tee, so she immediately knew that it wasn't part of the script. When Fr Pat started off the singing, she thought it was just a lovely contibution from him.

When a recording of the event at Trish and Neil's wedding ceremony was posted on social media, it went viral, with more than two million views in the first few days.

So Trish became 'an internet sensation' – something I have yet to achieve!

CHAPTER 11

THOUSANDS
FOR TEA

Wherever I travel around the globe, I never miss the opportunity to paint a picture of my own wonderful part of the world, County Donegal, and its breathtaking beauty.

It's my haven. It's my retreat. That's where I disappear to after a long concert tour to recharge my batteries. I return to my roots to walk the hills or fill my lungs with the pure sea air.

Through the decades, coming back from a long stint on tour, the magnificent view of the Donegal landscape immediately rejuvenated me. From the very beginning I knew I would never lose my grip on reality once I maintained that contact with the place and the people who helped to make me the type of person I am today.

It's not that I had any fear of my personality ever changing, but my family, neighbours and friends from my early days around Kincasslagh ensured that I kept my feet firmly on the ground.

It's still great to go back there, and just be plain Daniel Bosco 'from up the road'. Just like the old days when I was a youngster growing up there, I can saunter up the road and drop in unexpectedly on the neighbours. We chat about old times, and my career will rarely be the main thrust of the conversation.

The people up in that neck of the woods are not the type to be impressed by stardom. I know they're proud that one of their own has achieved so much, and it doesn't have to be stated.

Of all the awards that I've received – I'm lucky enough to have received many – the one I treasure most is the trophy that marks my selection as 'Donegal Person of the Year' in 1989. That was a tremendous honour for me because it came from the people and the county that I hold dear to my heart.

The citation read: 'Daniel O'Donnell is a perfect example to the youth of our county and country. Success has not gone to his head. He has never forgotten his roots. He has not forgotten his mother and his family. He has not forgotten his beloved Kincasslagh and Donegal. And, above all, he has not forgotten the people who have put him where he is today – his loyal fans. He is never too busy to stay behind after shows to talk to them and sign autographs. Many are the stories that could be told of his visits to homes and hospitals to visit sick fans, even when this meant interrupting busy schedules. One story which aptly displays his concern for his fans is the one which tells of an occasion when it came to his notice that some fans who were itinerants were being refused admittance to his show. He refused to go on stage until they were admitted. Daniel never loses an opportunity to lend his name and his services, if possible, to worthwhile charities. A non-drinker and non-smoker, his clean-cut image in his dress and in his living standards does not meet with approval from some of the gurus in the media, who seem to wish he were otherwise. But they meet with the approval of us here in Cumann Tir Chonaill (County Donegal).'

The people who select the Donegal Person of the Year felt that I was a great ambassador for the county on my travels and in my videos. The *Thoughts of Home* video includes many scenes of picturesque Donegal. But it's not that I've decided I'm going to do the job of the Irish tourist board. It's just that I'm so proud of my county that I want all my fans to come and see it. And to come and see Kincasslagh, where I grew up.

During my concert tours I regularly told audiences that if they were ever in Kincasslagh they were welcome to drop in for a cup of tea and a biscuit.

The town of Dungloe, which is a short run by car from Kincasslagh, has an annual festival called 'Mary From Dungloe', which has been running since 1968.

It's a great excuse for a full week of partying and has been attracting crowds of fifty thousand or more into the area. It's like the Rose of Tralee, with girls representing many countries taking part in the 'Mary' contest.

There is week-long dancing to top Irish bands and there's street music and everything else that goes with summer festivals of that ilk. I love being part of the whole event and I would usually do a number of shows in Dungloe that week.

In the months leading up to it, I would remind fans right across Britain and elsewhere that I'd be at home during that week if they wished to call and see me. And I always nominated a day that they were guaranteed to meet me.

In 1992, a total of three thousand people queued for hours along a narrow rural road leading to my home.

I was flabbergasted. I couldn't comprehend why people would queue for up to five hours to see ME. After all, I'm not in Loretta Lynn's league. But that's exactly what happened. My sister Kathleen and her merry band of helpers were busy that day dishing out the cups of tea! It's okay, she's still talking to me.

Some members of the Irish media who turned up to witness the strange event in a remote part of Ireland at the end of July later commented that it looked like the type of scene you might expect to find outside the home of a faith healer. Well, I'm no faith healer. I have no powers like that. And nobody asked me for a cure. They just wanted to shake my hand, have a quick chat and, in most cases, a souvenir photograph of the brief meeting.

I was overwhelmed by the number who came to see me. They came from the thirty-two counties of Ireland. They were there from England, Scotland and Wales. And there was even a lady who travelled over from the Falklands.

I suppose fans like to catch me in my natural environment. They normally see me on stage when I'm Daniel O'Donnell – The Performer. The 'open day' at my home gave them the opportunity to judge me away from the spotlight. I wasn't dressed the way they'd normally see me during a performance. I didn't even shave on the day. The saw me in a relaxed, homely atmosphere.

A wonderful aspect of the day, which then became an annual event, was that all the people there met new people. I encountered Catholics and Protestants from Northern Ireland who were travelling together and that was great to see. It's wonderful that there are no barriers when it comes to music and entertainment. That people can be united through their common love of song and dance.

My own neighbours around Kincasslagh dropped in and mingled with the visitors and I was pleased with that, as I felt guilty about the numbers I attracted into the area. I often wondered if I had interrupted the private lives of the locals and opened this remote part of the world to something that should not have been. But I don't think so.

The devotion of fans was just incredible. I recall reading one story about a woman from Northern Ireland who had set up a mini-shrine to me in her home. She had every tape I ever made and all the videos. And she had a scrapbook full of stuff about me. And mugs and cups I'd drunk from. She said that when she would eventually be called to meet the good Lord, she planned to be interred with one hundred photographs, wall charts and calendars of me, plus a flower I gave her, which she had pressed and preserved, and a bow-tie that I wore on stage. The story claimed she had given strict instructions to that effect to her bemused minister and family!

A question I'm often asked is, 'Why, unlike other performers, do you stay on for hours after a concert meeting the people who go to your shows? Is it not a terrible ordeal for you?'

I can only smile at such a suggestion. What many people in showbusiness can't understand is that meeting the fans after a concert is one of the most satisfying aspects of my career. It's not gruelling for me. I love meeting people and it helps me to wind down and relax after a couple of hours on the stage.

Because I don't drink, I have no interest in rushing off to the bar or to a trendy nightclub. That's not my style. I love people. I love being with them. And I think that that can be attributed to my roots in Donegal. Everyone around my area as a child ran an open house and there was a lot of interaction between neighbours.

Naturally, because I meet so many people at the one time, I don't get to know a large number of them very well. But there are some that I'm very familiar with because I would see them at four or five shows (and in some cases nearly every show) during the same tour. There are people who travel hundreds of miles to my shows. I'm sure some of them clock up thousands of miles following me every year. I'm very fortunate to possess a really sharp memory, so I can recall a lot of people when I meet them again.

But if you asked me what it is about me that can command such devotion, I wouldn't be able to tell you. I don't dwell on it. I don't question it. I have never tried to analyse it. I'm just happy that there are people out there who like what I do and the way that I do it.

***

Back in 1992, the Irish journalist and author Eddie Rowley, who has worked with me on this book, spoke to some of the visitors who called to my home in Kincasslagh during that year's 'open day' on 30 July. He wanted to hear their personal stories and the reasons why they were following me to the ends of the earth … or in this case Kincasslagh.

This is what they told him.

SHEILA DALZELLE – CUMBRIA

I had a very serious car accident back in 1985. It left me semi-disabled and unable to work. My world had collapsed around me. Then I discovered Daniel and life took on a whole new meaning again. I was always very fond of Irish music and I used to have tapes sent over to me from Ireland. One day a tape of Daniel O'Donnell arrived and from then on there was no one but Daniel for me. His music is very soothing and I got a lot of comfort from it. And, to me, Daniel was a bonus when I first met him. He was so nice and so friendly. He has filled in a big gap in my life. He has helped me to do things that I don't think I would have had the courage to do otherwise. I wouldn't have travelled long distances on a bus or train, for instance. But Daniel gave me the courage and motivation to do that because I knew he was going to be at the other end. Now I go on the bus down to London, which is a long way from where I live. Before that, I hadn't the confidence to travel. So, I have gained a lot of strength just from knowing Daniel and his music. He has visited me at my home and I just think that Daniel is everything that is right. Whenever I'm feeling down, I put on one of Daniel's videos, pull up a chair to the television and then I'm oblivious to everything around me. Daniel has helped me to accept what has gone wrong in my life. I had always wanted to take a trip on Concorde. So, in 1989, when I finally made up my mind to do it, I took Daniel to dinner on Concorde! And we had a ball. It was my way of saying thanks for everything he has done for me.

ROSE ORRIS – ESSEX

I first heard Daniel O'Donnell's music on Radio 2 in England and I immediately fell in love with it. My youngest boy bought me one of Daniel's videos for Mother's Day. Daniel was marvellous in it, so I went out and bought all his tapes and videos. Then I joined his Fan Club and found out where all his concerts were on. Now, my husband, Tony, and I go to as many of his concerts as we can. We often travel two hundred miles on public transport just for one show. But it's worth it because he's such an exciting performer and he gives us so much pleasure. We are both totally hooked on his music now. This is our very first trip to Ireland and we travelled all the way over by car, even though my husband only started driving three weeks ago! We wanted to see Daniel in Ireland and nothing would stop us. My son, Stephen, did a lovely portrait of Daniel, which we have framed and we have given it to Daniel as a present for his new home.

THORA ALAZIA – THE FALKLANDS

I heard Daniel O'Donnell's music for the first time just after the conflict and I thought it was wonderful. I immediately joined his Fan Club and I got all his cassettes. He has a lovely voice and his music is beautiful. All my walls are now plastered with Daniel's pictures. He's very pleasant on the eye. And I have travelled over eight thousand miles to Ireland to see him. Everywhere you go in the Falklands, you hear Daniel's music being played. People are going to be really envious when I tell them that I've met Daniel. Daniel is all that I ever thought he would be ... and more. He's such a friendly young man. I'll never forget this visit to Ireland, even if I never get back again. It will be the one thing that I'll always carry with me.

ANNE RONAN – GWENT

I started going to see Daniel O'Donnell in concert in 1987 and he was such an exciting performer. He brought me so much joy. Later, when I was diagnosed as having multiple sclerosis, Daniel was very kind and very caring to me. And we have become great friends. Even though I'm incapacitated, I follow him everywhere. I have wonderful friends who take me to his shows all over Britain. On his last tour, I saw eighteen of his twenty-five shows. I follow him to Scotland, England, Wales, Cornwall, Ireland – he's my whole life now. One day, I saw a van pulling up outside my home. I couldn't believe my eyes. It was Daniel. He was on his way to a concert in Cardiff and he called to see me. That day will never be taken out of my life. He said, 'Where's the tea, Anne?' I kept saying, 'I can't believe you're here!' He made his own tea, bless his heart. We had a little chat and off he trotted. I don't think I'll ever forget it. That's the kind of person Daniel is. People don't realise what he does behind the scenes. He has a heart of gold.

***

What I loved about the open day is that it brought people together and friendships were established. But ultimately we had to stop hosting that event, as it became too big to handle in terms of crowds and traffic around that small rural community. Towards the end I was only getting to see a fraction of the crowd and I feared that the fans were ultimately going to be disappointed with the experience.

Nevertheless it remains an incredible memory for me.

CHAPTER 12

TV AND
LORETTA LYNN

There was a time in the early days when I felt that television didn't serve me well.

I firmly believe that back then there was a large section of the Irish population that regarded Daniel O'Donnell as a boring performer who stood in the one spot on stage throughout his entire show.

They probably thought that I didn't move for fear of disturbing my hair or ruffling my clothes. Some of them may have believed that I was brain-dead and that I was some kind of robot who was programmed to sing.

But they had probably never been to a Daniel O'Donnell live show. Their impression of me had been formed from my TV appearances. And, in a way, I wouldn't have blamed them for having that kind of view of me.

In those early days I felt that television never adequately projected the type of stage show that I was bringing to life. And that was mainly due to the fact that most of my TV exposure in those times was studio work.

On the other hand, I considered myself very lucky to get the opportunity to appear on television as I was building up my career. Television definitely sprinkles you with magic dust. There's no doubt that TV boosted my career in Britain and the States when I was starting out. It was great to get the opportunity to appear on shows like *Wogan* and Val Doonican's show in the UK, and on the likes of *Nashville Now* in the States.

But I used to feel that I came across as a wax dummy or a plastic figure. It's very hard to project an overall image of what you're about when you have to operate on one spot in a TV studio. My attitude would change later in life, but I wasn't fan of doing television in those times.

It's ironic then that I got offered an incredible amount of TV way back then and still do to this day. Of course, today I thoroughly enjoy the experience, as I will later recount.

My break into 'big time' TV in Ireland arrived in 1989 when I was asked to host a 'special' show featuring country music. It was called *Country Comes Home* and it starred one of my favourite American country singers, Charley Pride, a performer I had first seen in action at the Wembley Country Music Festival in 1979. Charley really inspired me on that occasion, so it was a thrill to work with him on the TV show. The 'special' also saw the appearance of that wonderful mother and daughter duo The Judds. Despite my reservations about doing it, *Country Comes Home* was a big success, attracting high ratings and critical acclaim.

One break can often lead to another, and I was then offered my own TV series, *The Daniel O'Donnell Show*.

People who know me well will tell you I'm a cool customer. I'm so laid-back at times, I'm almost stretched out on the ground. That's just the way I am. I don't have to work at it. I don't need any form of therapy or sporting activity or drugs to help me cope with the stress that goes with a high-rolling career. By nature, I can take on an awful lot of pressure and handle it quite well.

Doing television work can be very stressful, particularly when it's not your natural environment and it's a totally new set of circumstances to have to handle. Hosting a long-running TV series was a new ball game for me. I basically had to come to terms with a new skill overnight. And even though I didn't particularly like the medium at the time, I think I handled it well and did a competent job.

That show's producer and director, John McColgan, said that I took direction very well. In a newspaper interview he acknowledged that his respect for me had grown throughout the series because I was able to memorise the complex instructions that he dished out and get the lines and actions right first time. I probably do have a photographic memory and I'm very visual. I just have to take one look at the layout of a stage before a show and I know where every item of equipment is situated when I'm performing. So I never have to look at the ground.

The Daniel O'Donnell Show was a ten-week series of one-hour shows, featuring over forty national and international guests. They included American stars Loretta Lynn, Lorrie Morgan, Ed Bruce, The Forrester Sisters and Stella Parton.

There was also a huge line-up of Irish artistes, including The Dubliners,

Foster and Allen, Philomena Begley, Susan McCann, Ray Lynam, Margo, Mary Duff, Dominic Kirwan, Mick Flavin and Bridie Gallagher. I was very happy with the series and it also gave me the opportunity to fulfil a life-long ambition – to perform with my idol, Loretta Lynn, the Coal Miner's Daughter.

There are a number of fans whom I meet on a regular basis during my concert tours. Some of them I know well because I encounter them so often, and I find it strange when they're nervous in my presence. Off-stage, I'm no different to anyone else. I don't put on any kind of big act to create an aura around me. I'm just a normal guy, so it really was a mystery to me as to why they react in that way. That is, until the day I met Loretta Lynn, and I became a nervous wreck myself.

I don't know if a person can actually say at the end of their day, 'The best day of my life was ...' I don't know if that is possible. But the day I met Loretta Lynn goes down in my book as one of the highlights of my life. A moment to be treasured forever. I still get goosebumps when I think about it.

Loretta Lynn has always been the one country singer that I've been totally devoted to. My love affair with lovely Loretta began the day I was introduced to her music by my sister Margaret. It's very difficult for me to define exactly what it was about Loretta that plucked at my heart strings above any other country singer. I suppose it's her incredible voice. A voice that makes you pulse with excitement. No other artiste has ever made the same impression on me.

I'll never forget the first time I met Loretta. It was way back in 1984 at the Wembley Country Music Festival. That festival sure does bring back a lot of good memories for me. I remember that I was casually strolling around the merchandise stands between shows – the area was like Grand

Central Station and I got carried along in the colourful crowd.

I'm a great people-watcher and I was totally engrossed by the different characters, some of whom were dressed as cowboys for the day, while others had come along as Indian chiefs. It's all part of the fun of the occasion, an excuse for otherwise normal people – accountants, solicitors, shop assistants and the like – to act out their harmless fantasies. I hardly noticed the lady who was surrounded by an excited group, with individuals clamouring for her attention. Who was creating all the fuss?

As I got closer I realised: My God, it's Loretta Lynn.

Right there before my eyes.

Almost within touching distance.

Loretta Lynn! Loretta Lynn! My heart started thumping against my chest. This was the singer I had idolised for years. Loretta Lynn! I was like a child waking up on Christmas morning to find his dream toy beside him. Christmas had arrived early for me.

I wanted to race out and tell the whole of London that Loretta Lynn was in Wembley Arena and that she was right there in front of me, signing autographs for people. Loretta Lynn! I had been with some friends from Scotland, but we had become separated in the crowd. So I frantically raced around looking for them. Eventually, I located them near the area where we were seated.

I was breathless at this stage and I could only gulp: 'L-L-Loretta Lynn! Loretta L-L-Lynn is out there and she's signing autographs!'

I wanted them to see her too.

I wanted everyone to see this wonderful woman.

I went back to the stand and I just stood there before her in the crowd, mesmerised. I was in a trance-like state. She was still signing autographs.

Now, I was never an autograph-hunter, but if getting an autograph was the only way I was going to get closer to Loretta Lynn and, my God, even speak to her, then suddenly I had a huge interest in autographs. But how was I going to compose myself to make the approach? My legs were buckling under me at the very thought of it.

It seemed like I was there for hours. And as the time ticked away I was no nearer to getting my act together and I almost let the opportunity slip by. But as she was about to depart, I suddenly found myself racing up to her. And, like a dog chasing a bus, I didn't know what to do when I caught up with her. I just blurted out: 'God, I love you!'

Loretta Lynn turned to me and smiled. She smiled at me, Daniel O'Donnell from Kincasslagh, County Donegal. And she whispered: 'Thank you, honey.' She gave me a kiss and then she was gone. Well, talk about being high, I could have flown back home to Donegal without wings! It took me weeks to come down from whatever planet I was on.

In 1988 when I went to Nashville to appear at the Fan Fair extravaganza, I went along to see Loretta Lynn's home which is open to the public. I was still carrying the torch for Loretta. And actually being inside her home was an incredible experience. Touching the table where she had her meals. The chair where she relaxed in the evening when she wasn't away on tours.

Loretta, unfortunately, wasn't home when I called. But when I returned to Ireland, I sent Loretta Lynn the only fan mail I have ever written in my life. I wrote and told her how much her music meant to me. And I recall finishing off the letter with a line that went something like, 'Whenever you are feeling down, I just want you to remember that there are thousands of people like me who have a friendly kind of love for you.'

Little did I know then that our paths were to cross a year later. Fate was about to smile on Daniel yet again, because Loretta had been lined up to appear on my show. God, I have an awful lot of favours to pay off. A lot is expected of the man who is given a lot.

The day in 1989 Loretta Lynn was due into Ireland, you would think to look at me that it was my wedding day. 'Mr Cool' had suddenly lost his composure. I was up at the break of dawn, hopping around the place like an expectant father. I was totally flustered. I couldn't sit down and relax. I had to keep on the move to occupy my mind.

Isn't it amazing the influence that one individual can have over another? I know there are people who will tell me that that is how I affect them. I find the way I react to Loretta quite incredible, just as I am always surprised by the reaction of people to me.

My itinerary for the day included a trip to Dublin Airport to greet Loretta personally and welcome her to the country. But when the time arrived for me to go out in the car, I got cold feet. I lost my nerve. I just couldn't summon up the courage to go out and meet the woman that I was absolutely devoted to. I made some excuse and got out of the trip. My friends will be surprised by this, because I normally take things in my stride.

But I wasn't off the hook. Like it or not, the moment would arrive when I would have no other option but to meet Loretta. Worse still, I had to sing with her and interview her during the show. While I was thrilled at the prospect of that, I was also terrified that I might go to pieces.

Some time earlier, I had been told a story about an Irish photographer who was commissioned to photograph Johnny Cash and one of our own country singers, Sandy Kelly, when the two performed together in Ireland. Sandy's then manager Kieran Cavanagh, who now looks after me, had booked the photographer but didn't realise that he was a lifetime fan of

Johnny Cash. When the moment finally arrived for the arranged picture to be taken backstage at a show and Johnny Cash walked into the room, the photographer fainted in front of his eyes. It was too much for the poor man, meeting his idol in the flesh. There was no photograph taken that night.

I had an awful vision of something like that happening to me as soon as I found myself in the presence of Loretta.

The following day I was up at the crack of dawn because it was the day that the show was due to be recorded. There was no breakfast for me that morning either – sure I wouldn't have been able to keep it down.

Later in the day while I was in my dressing room at the TV studios, the sound of that wonderful voice drifted in. It was Loretta next door in her dressing room. Well, I was like something that had been wrapped in tinfoil all my life and had been just opened up. My tummy was going into spasms. My legs hadn't the power to carry my body next door to say 'Hi.' People were telling me that Loretta had arrived, so I had to pretend that I was busy doing something while I tried to gather my wits. There was a Walkman on the dressing table, so I put on the ear-phones and pretended I was listening to it. Afterwards, I discovered that there wasn't even a tape in the machine!

Eventually, I made the supreme effort and walked next door to her dressing room. You'd think I was going to the electric chair to look at me. Loretta was everything I had imagined her to be ... and more. She was a stunning-looking woman, with piercing blue eyes, Cherokee cheekbones and hair the colour of coal. She gave me a big hug, and I felt I was going to die. I had the feeling of being in the presence of someone special. And Loretta is someone special.

My rise to stardom from humble beginnings pales into insignificance by comparison with Loretta's achievements. She grew up in Butcher Hollow,

Kentucky, dirt-poor and isolated. She was married at thirteen, a mother at fourteen, and by the age of eighteen she had four of her six children. At thirty-two, Loretta was a millionaire. At thirty-four, she was a grand-mother. It is said that she had a tough time with her husband, Doolittle as she calls him, who early on succumbed to the demon booze and was also a womaniser. The story of her incredible life, warts and all, was chronicled in the film *Coal Miner's Daughter*.

My mother had been to see the film, and during Loretta and Doolittle's visit to Ireland for my show, she cornered Doolittle. 'You were a right boyo!', my mother told him, putting the fear of God into him. The poor man thought his time had come. She was a very formidable lady, my mother.

Loretta Lynn has been a great inspiration to artistes like myself. What she has achieved without an education, and despite being a child bride and penniless, has given other performers hope and drive to strive for our goals. It was a great privilege to perform with Loretta and to be given the opportunity to speak with her.

I relaxed once we started working together in the studio, and the inter-view went very well. When it was all over and Loretta had returned home to America I had to pinch myself every now and then to be sure that it hadn't been a dream. I never thought then that Loretta would be back to see me one day – and this time in my own native Kincasslagh.

For many years the Donegal Shore Festival committee in Kincasslagh organised a special event where they surprised me with a well-known guest – my belle for the night – who meant something to me. My sister Kathleen played a major role in this showpiece of the festival and it was always a well-guarded secret. I never knew who was going to be by my side until the blindfold was removed. Among the surprise belles over the years were

Ireland's first Eurovision winner, Dana, TV and radio personality Gloria Hunniford and *Coronation Street* star Liz Dawn (Vera Duckworth).

I never, ever, thought for a split second that one day it would be Loretta Lynn, but Kathleen and everyone on the committee made that happen in the autumn of 1997!

In July of that year I had actually met Loretta when I went to see her perform in a barn-style theatre beside her home in America. It was the first time I had seen the living legend perform a full concert, and it was an incredible experience for me. After the show I queued up with the rest of the audience to have a quick word when she was signing autographs.

Eventually I reached the head of the queue and I said, 'Loretta, do you remember Daniel?'

To be honest, I didn't expect her to remember me as it had been eight years since we last met on my TV show.

'Honey! Oh my God!' she exclaimed showing instant recognition. Then she gave me a big hug.

'What are you doing, honey? Can I meet you later?' Loretta then asked.

Unfortunately I had a flight to catch back to Ireland at the time.

When I told her this, Loretta said to her manager, 'Lane, aren't we ...'

She had obviously forgotten the secrecy surrounding the Kincasslagh festival event. I learned later that her manager Lane was behind me and waving furiously at Loretta not to let the cat out of the bag. So Loretta never finished the sentence and I was none the wiser.

I told her I would be back again in August and I would go to her show and meet up then. As it turned out, I didn't make that date due to my own work commitments.

Fast-forward to that autumn, and I'm standing in the festival dome in

Kincasslagh wondering what vision is going to greet me when they remove my blindfold. Well, I instantly turned into an emotional, sobbing mess when I saw Loretta standing there before me, wearing an emerald green-and-gold dress and a beaming smile. People told me that the blood drained from my face, and I remember feeling faint. Then I broke down and cried, which was a bit embarrassing but people who knew how crazy I was about Loretta totally understood my reaction.

Loretta was very funny that night. She told the audience about my visit to her concert and how I promised I'd return.

'He said he would come in August. I hollered out at my show, "Daniel O'Donnell have you sneaked in here again without telling me?"'

We danced that night in Kincasslagh and then I left the ball with my belle and accompanied Loretta on her journey by car to Dublin as she had an early morning flight back home. It was a pure joy to be with her. Loretta talked non-stop from the time we got into the car until we arrived in Dublin city. Then we had an early morning breakfast in a hotel, and all too soon it was time to say goodbye.

The hours in Loretta's company had passed in a flash, but they will stay with me forever.

Days and nights like that are what dreams are made of.

Later I would strike up a close friendship with another of my idols … Cliff Richard.

CHAPTER 13

CONQUERING THE
MOUNTAIN

1992 was a very strange year for me. It was a very uncertain year. It was a year when I discovered more about myself than I had done in the previous ten.

This started on 1 January, with a dramatic phone call to my manager, Sean Reilly.

During a brief conversation, I said to him, 'Sean, I'm worried about my voice. I need to speak to you.'

He immediately said, 'Come over.'

And I knew before I left what I was going to do. I had decided to go off the road. I went to Sean and told him I needed to take a break. He asked, 'How long?', and I said it would probably be about six months. I had decided that following the advice of my voice specialist, Tom Wilson.

As I have said earlier, of all the people that I could have teamed up with management-wise, I'm very lucky to have found Sean Reilly. There's a great human element to Sean. His immediate response to my decision to put my career on ice for six months was, 'That's fine. Leave it with me.' There was no haggling over the amount of time I was planning to take off. No pressure from Sean to fulfil the concert dates that I was already committed to and for which a large number of tickets had been sold. Sean's only concern was for my welfare. That's the calibre of the man I had as my manager. He's a rare species in the showbiz world and, believe me, I never took that for granted.

I left Sean that day with a sense of relief. A burden had been lifted from my shoulders, because I knew I couldn't do it anymore. But there was also the awful realisation that it was all over for me. Although I've always said I knew I was going to come back, I have to admit now that for a while I really thought it was the end.

In a short period of six years, I had made an incredible leap forward in the showbiz world. From being virtually unknown and struggling to secure dates even in my own country, I had reached a stage where I was a major concert attraction in Britain and Ireland, with my albums and videos selling hundreds of thousands of copies. But you don't achieve that level of success without paying some kind of price. And I almost paid the ultimate. I was physically exhausted.

My thirtieth birthday, on 12 December 1991, was one of the worst days of my life. I did a concert in Letterkenny, County Donegal. It should have been super, but my throat was sore, I was exhausted, I just couldn't cope with it. People will probably be shocked to discover that I was feeling that way. I was very near to total exhaustion. I suppose the signs had been there for a long time. I had been irritable. I mentioned earlier about having a short fuse and at times I would blow up with members of the band or other people on the road with me.

When I look back, I realise now that the pressure was getting to me. I knew that there was something wrong with me. I felt it in The Galtymore in London's Cricklewood in the middle of my British tour. I had it on 12 December. I definitely had it in The Beaten Path, Claremorris, County Mayo, on 26 December. And I don't ever want to experience that kind of exhaustion again. I had to cancel a show the night after The Beaten Path. I wasn't able to sing. I wasn't able to talk.

When I woke up on the morning of 29 December, I was still exhausted. And I had a show ahead of me that night in the Cush Inn, Kildangan, County Kildare. I decided to go ahead with it. But during the performance I knew that every song I sang was getting closer to the one that was going to be the last.

I told the audience that night when I went on stage at The Cush Inn that I had a sore throat, that I didn't know how long I was going to sing for. Then later on that night, after I had been on for about an hour, it was very near stopping time. Eventually, I wasn't able to sing anymore. It was the strangest sensation.

I had pushed myself too much. I was all things to everybody and nothing to myself. When I took a break during the show, I asked my personal assistant Joe Collum to ring Sean and ask him to cancel everything that was coming up before our planned holiday on 6 January. I went back on stage and told the audience a couple of jokes. I didn't sing very much after that because with the passing minutes my throat got progressively worse and eventually it wasn't working at all. I don't know if the audience were aware of how I was feeling because I was always very good at concealing my form. But they gave me a standing ovation as I left the stage.

I was very lucky that I stopped when I did. It was either stop the bus or go around the corner and crash. I was my own worst enemy. There was nobody at any time driving me too hard. Why did I feel I had to do so much? Because so much was put to me. When you get a letter from some-body who's a lot worse off than you – I don't mean financially – it's very hard to turn around and say, 'Well, I can't do anything about that.'

I had been thinking about stopping for some time before I did. But I used to think: How can I stop? The majority of the people in the band are married. What are they going to do? What about all the concerts that are sold out? And so on. But that line of thinking is ludicrous and stupid, because if you are no good to yourself, you are no good to anybody.

And that's what I realised at the end of December.

In early January 1992, I went off on a pre-arranged holiday to Orlando, Florida, taking my young nephews and nieces to Disneyland. While I was relaxing down there, news reached me from home that there were some strange stories circulating about my health, the most grotesque being that I had throat cancer and would never sing again.

Looking back, my pre-planned holiday was a blessing in disguise. I avoided all the fuss surrounding my 'illness'. The newspapers were full of it. And poor old Sean was inundated with queries from journalists. There was even a story in showbiz circles that I had orchestrated the whole saga so that I could get rid of my band without having to sack them. Needless to say, all those stories were without foundation.

When I arrived back at Dublin Airport after a gruelling flight, during which I thought we were all going to die because the turbulence was so severe, there were even media people waiting for me at Arrivals. I had never experienced that before in Ireland. Sickness is obviously bigger news than singing.

Back home, I now had time to take stock of my situation. I felt a terrible emptiness as the full impact of what had just happened to me began to sink in. I had been on top of the world. But now the rug had been pulled from under my feet and I was in 'no man's land'. My voice had gone. My career had gone, at least temporarily.

I felt at that time that my purpose in life had gone. I didn't even have a home. Before Christmas 1991, I sold my house on the southside of Dublin city. I was in the process of buying another residence on the Dublin–Kildare border. But the deal hadn't gone through. So, I now found myself in a rented apartment in Dublin. Alone, and in strange surroundings, I was really feeling sorry for myself. I was like a fish out of water. I had never really been out of work. Even though times were hard in the beginning, the drive to succeed was always there to motivate me.

Now it seemed that all that had changed.

During the days and weeks that followed, I came to terms with my new lifestyle and set about the task of rebuilding my physical strength. I started working out in a gym to get back into shape – and I hated every minute of it. Despite my best efforts, I never got close to giving Arnold Schwarzenegger a run for his money.

I started doing all the things I never got the opportunity to do when I was working. Things like going to the theatre, dancing, and playing whist and ten-pin bowling. I went along to see other singers perform. And I was contributing my weekly column to the Irish newspaper *Sunday World*. So, a routine gradually began to develop. My days were starting earlier. Instead of getting out of bed in the afternoon, as I did when I was working, I started getting up around the same time as everyone else.

For about a year before I had to finally throw in the towel, I was attending a Dublin throat specialist, Tom Wilson. I had never been formally trained as a singer. So Tom took me back through the basics. He taught me how to sing from the diaphragm and not just the larynx. I'm not saying he has turned me into a Pavarotti or a Carreras. I'm neither of those and I never will be. I haven't got the perfect technique for singing and I still get a little hoarse from time to time when I sing. But I don't get as hoarse as I used to and I can sing above it. So, Tom played a big role in getting me back on the stage again.

But physically, I was still feeling dreadful. I kept saying to people, 'I have something wrong with me!' I went to doctors. They carried out all kinds of tests on me. 'Nothing wrong. Nothing wrong,' they told me. But I insisted that there was a tightness in my chest. I blew into every tube there was to blow into, but they couldn't find anything.

Eventually, I went to a herbalist, Sean Boylan. He discovered that my diaphragm was out of position. He stretched me and I could hear the crack as he rectified the problem. Then he gave me herbal medicine, which I really feel helped me a lot too.

One day I heard a healing priest called Fr Rookey being interviewed on the radio in Dublin by broadcaster Pat Kenny, and I felt I should see him. Fr Rookey told his own story that morning. He had been blinded in both eyes as a child in Chicago. After being told that doctors could do nothing for him, he went on to make a miraculous recovery. I eventually went to a Mass he celebrated in London's Acton Town Hall and joined people to receive his blessing. When he touched my forehead I fell to the floor. And I firmly believe that Fr Rookey played a huge part in my recovery.

At Fr Rookey's Mass I met a nun from Donegal called Sr Philomena. When I told her the reason I was there, Sr Philomena reached into her bag and took out healing prayers. She said: 'Something told me to put these prayers in my bag today and now I know they are for you.'

I went to every faith healer who was mentioned to me at that time. I wasn't going to leave anything to chance. I attended a healer in Dublin called Joe Dalton. Joe told me a story about problems he'd had in his own life. He said: 'I spent my time questioning and saying why am I like this, why have I got this turmoil, why can I not do what I want to do? And then one night I sat down and said, "Right God, if you want me to do something I'll do it. If I am not meant to work at what I am doing then I'll happily stop, but I need to know."'

I heard what I needed in that statement. I thought, 'If I have to not sing, I need a reason for not doing it. I'm giving it over to God to be sorted out, because I can't handle this.' A few days later I woke up feeling a lot better. I actually remember thinking, I feel better today. I felt that something had released me. So, through a combination of all those faith healers and treatments – I also went to a homeopath in Castlebar, Co Mayo, by the name of Kevin Barrett and took some medicines that he gave me – I eventually got better.

***

I had the support of very good friends during this difficult time. One of my great friends in life has been a lady called Josephine Burke, who lives outside the city of Dublin. Just like Sean Reilly, Josephine has been a rock of support to me throughout my life.

Josephine is married and has her own family life, but I could never spend enough time with her because she brought me such joy. All through the years she was my confidante, my psychologist and my rock. She is a good listener and she doesn't tell me any lies.

I first met Josephine in 1973, when I was only eleven years old. She was a friend of my sister, Margaret. Josephine and a group of her friends were fans of Margaret and used to regularly attend her shows all over the country. Later when we became friends I realised the value of having a genuinely good friend in my life. A good friend is better than all the success in the world. That kind of friendship is worth a fortune.

My best friend at home in Donegal is still P.J. Sweeney. We have been friends since schooldays, but our friendship was firmly established when we went off on a foreign holiday together one time. Time spent with somebody tends to make or break a friendship, and P.J. and I got on very well together on that holiday. We went to the Greek island of Crete and had a wonderful time – we never stopped laughing.

I remember one night we were out enjoying the entertainment and we noticed two girls throwing shapes on the dancefloor. We decided to join them. We pretended we couldn't speak English and we danced with the two women, who were also on holidays. In fact, we danced with them several nights after that, maintaining our pose as 'foreigners'. Then one day we met them on the street and P.J. forgot himself and said, 'How's it goin'?'

Strangely enough, they carried on a conversation with us without any reference to our act!

On that holiday P.J. and I hired out a little scooter and that was hilarious. P.J. is over six feet tall and weighed about fifteen stone – well, the poor little scooter was huffing and puffing trying to go up a hill. I had to get off because it didn't have the power to carry the two of us.

That was a great carefree holiday in my early years that I'll always remember. P.J. became my best friend in life, and he's someone I would trust with my life. I think it is really important for everyone in showbusiness to stay close to their families and friends. They are the people who will keep you on the straight and narrow if you are the sort of person who might lose touch with reality.

There are people who put me up on a pedestal. They seem to think that I'm some kind of saintly figure and that I don't have faults like they do – that what they do, I would never do. But I'm really no different to anyone else. I have my bad moments, the same as the next person.

If people stayed around long enough, they would hear me letting out the odd swear word. I have a wicked sense of humour at times, and like many others I can sometimes see the funny side of another person's misfortune.

There are moments when I have a short fuse. And when my temper blows, I have a wild, sharp tongue. There would be no answer to what I might say. And in those circumstances, I'm not always right. Nobody is right all the time.

It's usually the people I think most of that I lose my temper with. People in the band. Family. Friends. You always hurt the ones you love. It would be instantaneous. And then it would be all forgotten just as quickly.

I suppose that comes as a surprise to most of my fans. They would be devastated if I lost my temper with them. They would feel that they were cut in two and that they'd never heal. It's not that I have a dreadful temper. But I do have a sharp tongue.

***

When my career was in jeopardy, I coped with the trauma by turning to God. As I have said, I believe I'm run-of-the-mill where religion is concerned. I'm not obsessive about it. It has always been important to me, but I don't consider myself to be over-religious. But during those dark days when I faced an uncertain future, I started to seek solace through my faith. And I began to think: Well, maybe there's something else HE wants me to do. Maybe there's another area I need to discover about myself. I sometimes mention that during my shows nowadays when I tell the audience how I'm very pleased that HE didn't want me to do something else.

During the early stages of my recuperation, I had decided that I would be able to return to the stage earlier than had been initially anticipated. With the advice of Tom Wilson, I decided to start back on 1 April. But as that date drew near, I was filled with a sense of foreboding. A fear of the unknown began to consume me. And, physically, I didn't feel an awful lot better. I hadn't been attending Sean Boylan for very long at that time, and this was before my visit to Fr Rookey.

During the last couple of weeks before that first concert at The Civic Centre in Halifax, I experienced bouts of panic. I was very, very nervous. On the big night, my system was in tatters. I wasn't functioning properly at all.

I don't know how I survived that night. Waiting in the wings to go on, the power left my legs. And when it was time for me to step out, those legs refused to carry me to the middle of the stage. I had to lean on a speaker to support myself. But when I heard the sound of my voice, my confidence gradually began to build up. After that, it was like climbing the ladder again. From then on, I progressed step by step, and those steps would lead me to my first major concert at Dublin's biggest arena.

CHAPTER 14

THE POINT

The Point Theatre in the Dublin docklands had played host to the big names in almost every category of music, from classical great José Carreras to country legend Don Williams and rock supergroup U2.

Early in 1992, my manager Sean Reilly and Irish promoter Kieran Cavanagh got together at Dublin's Mont Clare Hotel and hatched a plan for me to perform there on my 'comeback' in Ireland.

When Sean told me about it, I was hesitant at first. The Point, to me, was beyond my wildest aspirations. My dreams never included a concert at Ireland's biggest indoor arena. No Irish country singer had ever performed there as the main attraction.

People have often accused me of not taking risks, but this was certainly going into unknown territory. I have great faith in Sean, and eventually I said, 'If you think I can do it, then let's do it.' I felt that because he was confident that I could do it, I should be confident that he could make it a success.

It takes a lot of people to fill The Point Theatre, and I was apprehensive about how it would turn out. But Kieran Cavanagh is a professional and highly respected promoter. By then he had brought many of the big American country acts, including the great Johnny Cash, to Ireland on successful tours.

Kieran and Sean spent several months planning the big concert for me. The promotion wasn't just concentrated on Ireland; fans who come to see me in Britain were also notified about it through hand-bills distributed at the various venues. Travel packages by sea and air were organised and advertised. The technical side of my show also had to be revamped. We had never played that size of theatre before, so extra lighting and sound equipment was hired to ensure a proper impact.

The morning of Saturday, 11 July 1992 finally arrived and I was up at cockcrow. I couldn't sleep due to a combination of nerves and excitement.

I remember thinking: 'Jeez, I wish I had gone out to a dance last night. I would have slept later.'

Irish country singer Mick Flavin had been playing in Barry's Hotel the previous night, but I had resisted the temptation to go to that dance because I wanted to be bright and energetic for my own show. That day involved lots of trips to the loo. A big show is certainly a great cure for constipation! During the day I had a sound check, so that helped to pass away a couple of hours.

The band was in great shape. I had prepared my programme for the show three weeks previously and they had done a number of eight-hour days rehearsing it under the charge of my musical director, John Ryan. When he felt he had them at their peak, I was brought in. So, everything was sounding good for later that night.

It was a relief to discover on the night that there were over six thousand people in the theatre. Now it was up to me to do the rest.

As the overture was playing before I went out on stage, a wave of emotion swept through me. I think it was the realisation of just how far I had come in Ireland.

Playing to a full house at The Point Theatre was the pinnacle of my career at home. It was a big moment for me. So, I suppose I savoured that a little as I prepared to step out on the stage. But as soon as I appeared in front of the crowd, those feelings left me.

As I was singing 'The Rose of Tralee', I felt a great sense of pride that, at long last, so many Irish songs were being sung in The Point. The audience that night was wonderful. They were like a choir and I could hear them singing all night. They knew all the songs, especially the slow numbers which they could really get into.

Looking back, I feel my show at The Point helped to alter dramatically Irish people's image of me. I think I gained a lot of respect and admiration through my live performance that night.

There were a lot of people at the show who had never seen me in action before, except on TV. They had absolutely no idea about the content of the show. They probably expected to be bored by a guy who they thought would stand in the one spot all night singing. But, as my regular concert-goers know, there is a lot of energy in my live act.

Afterwards, one woman said to me, 'I've never seen you before,' and I don't know if she was asking me 'Why?' or asking herself 'Why?' And I suppose that is the nicest compliment anyone can give me.

A lot of people remarked on how I was leaping into the air and putting on a physically demanding performance. Many were surprised by the rock 'n' roll aspect of it, where I do a medley of Elvis hits, including 'That's All Right, Mama', 'Love Me Tender', 'Are You Lonesome Tonight?' and 'Don't Be Cruel'.

That's good for me because it's another form of expression and it's important for me to show people that there's more to me than just a white suit and a clean-cut image. There are also a lot of young people who come to see me and they like to see that kind of action.

The people who don't realise that I do have a sense of humour were surprised to hear me telling jokes and giving the odd bum-wiggle during my performance. But a show is made up of lots of elements and you lift people in different ways. With the songs. With the music. With the way you express yourself when you're speaking. And with your body movements.

I'm not trying to give the impression that I'm Tom Jones, although I did have a bra thrown at me during the show at The Point. It was the first time that that ever happened to me and I must admit it was a bit of a shock. The lady in question had put her name and address on the inside with a message asking me to send her a card. I duly obliged.

On stage, I'm very different. I'm much more outgoing and I'm much more assertive. There's a part of me for the stage that never comes out anywhere else. I'm totally at home and I feel I'm very confident when I'm up there.

I know that what I'm doing isn't everybody's cup of tea. But if you come along and see my show, I hope you will find that I do it on a very professional level and to the best of my ability. And if I feel it's going to do them any good, I will sometimes take other singers up on stage to perform at my shows. People often ask me why I do that. But it doesn't do me any harm to have new talent coming on the scene. I can only perform in one venue on any one night. There's plenty of room for everybody, plenty of success to go around.

On reflection, my concert at the Point Theatre – which is now known as the 3Arena – marked the beginning of a new era for me. My break from the scene allowed me to take a long, hard look at my career. And I realised that I could no longer continue giving so much of myself, both on and off the stage. Physically, it's just not possible to do it, as I discovered.

I realised that I pushed myself to the limit trying to do everything that was put to me. The pressure eventually brought me to my knees. If I was a drinker, I probably would have ended up an alcoholic. If I was into drugs, I hate to think what the consequences might have been. But I didn't have a crutch like that. And because I didn't have a crutch, I was standing straight all the time.

At the end, I was just high enough to see over the cloud to say that: 'This is awful. I need to clear this area.' I don't really know how long I had to clear it. But I believe now that I didn't have very long. I also held it all in. I tried not to show people just how tired I was feeling. And I suppose that takes more out of yourself, trying to give the impression that you're up when you're not up at all.

The pressure I brought upon myself was a result of the close contact I have with people. Because I was very accessible I was asked to do a lot of things outside of showbiz. There are numerous requests for private visits and I have always said, 'Sure, no problem.' I'm not saying I was some kind of Good Samaritan running to people every day of the week. But I did a lot of that behind the scenes.

Now, it's very hard for me to go and visit people and then do a show. It wasn't in the beginning. And that's what I couldn't understand. I was asking myself, 'Why am I so tired when I was actually doing more in the beginning?'

When I look at my first year with Ritz, I was out morning, noon and night. I wouldn't be physically capable of doing that now. I feel I have learned how to cope with a career at this level. I think I'm fairly well adjusted. In the early days, I had no time for myself. It wasn't healthy. That's something I had to rectify. But I still don't want to be locked away. I still want to meet people. That's important to me too.

I reorganised my show so that I didn't spend as much time on stage as I used to. Consequently, I felt my live performance was much better because I didn't become exhausted. I was certainly getting more enjoyment out of my concerts and the shows were attracting a wider range of people.

When I look at my life at that point, I realise that I had enjoyed more than I ever thought I would have the opportunity to do. But luckiest of all is that the success didn't smother me. It almost did, but after dealing with the burnout I was better adjusted for this life.

As I looked to the future, I was excited for the journey that lay ahead. I had a lot more living to do. A lot more performing. More people to meet from all walks of life. And, if I was lucky, maybe I would even meet a special person to share my life with.

After all, I was then only thirty years old.

CHAPTER 15

MAJELLA

As I set my life on a new track in 1992, some incredible events unfolded to really lift my spirits. I had my first big UK hit in the mainstream chart with the song 'I Just Want to Dance With You'. And that same week Donegal won the All-Ireland Senior Football Championship for the first time.

I will never forget that moment and the atmosphere in Croke Park as our team out-played 'the Dubs' (Dublin) to take home the coveted Sam Maguire Cup.

Getting the opportunity to perform 'I Just Want to Dance With You' on BBC's *Top of the Pops* TV chart show that week was like winning my very own All-Ireland. Back then, you really had 'arrived' as a singer if you made it onto that legendary show.

***

My career from 1992 on grew and grew, and six years later I was presented with an opportunity to give a little back. A neighbour of mine called Eileen Oglesby was involved in charity work with a Romanian orphanage, and she asked me to help out.

I decided to record a song called 'Give a Little Love' in aid of the charity. At that time, in 1998, I had no intention of getting directly involved in the relief work. But when I went to Romania to shoot a video for the song I was shocked by what I witnessed in the Siret orphanage.

It was heartbreaking to see children who had been totally deprived of love and human warmth and kindness. I saw boys and girls with their heads shaved, sleeping about 30 to a room. They were sitting around tables and just rocking back and forth.

Monica McDaid, the Irish woman in charge of the charity, said she found 1700 children at the home I was visiting when she arrived there in 1989. The majority of them were actually living in the basement with water flowing on the ground, rats were scurrying around the place, there was no heating … and two or three children were tied to each cot.

Monica explained that when Ceaucescu was in power, he had ordered that every family should have five children. But the parents simply couldn't afford to keep them, so they gave them up and they ended up in horror orphanages.

I knew during that visit to Romania that it was a scandal that needed someone to shine a light on it, and I felt that I was that someone when I came face to face with it. As an entertainer, I have a platform to speak out, and I was able to put a spotlight on those orphanages in Romania and encourage the people at the shows to donate money to the charity.

People were very generous and what was achieved as a result was just amazing. The money raised built houses and apartments and bought a farm. The people from the orphanage were integrated into the community, provided with livelihoods and allowed to become independent.

I will always be grateful for the fact that I was given an opportunity to help make a difference and to use my celebrity in a positive way. Anyone who gets that chance is fortunate and should take it.

***

They say that in the law of karma, whatever you give will come back to you. My own life had been blessed in so many ways. It had everything, with one exception: someone special to share it with. That would change following a trip to the beautiful holiday isle of Tenerife in the autumn of 1999.

I had been holidaying on the island since 1994 and had become friendly with an Irish couple, Tom and Marion Roche, who ran an Irish bar. As I normally did on my holidays, I dropped by their bar one evening with some friends shortly after I arrived. That night their daughter, Majella, was in the bar and we struck up a conversation. From the first moment of meeting we were totally at ease in each other's company. We laughed and laughed together all evening. On reflection I have no idea what we found so funny.

The fact that I was a well-known singer didn't have any impact at all on Majella, and neither should it have. Majella said in interviews later that she wasn't the type of person who had posters of her idols plastered across her bedroom walls as a teenager. Indeed, she had been used to rubbing shoulders with singers who were world superstars and legends in a previous job as head cashier at Wembley Stadium in London. She had met lots of celebrities up close, including Michael Jackson, Tina Turner, David Bowie and Diana Ross. That was a normal day for Majella. Sure compared to that, I was only in the ha'penny place!

As so often happens in an Irish gathering, there was a sing-song late in the night and I noticed Majella joining in. She had a very good voice. When I complimented her on her lovely singing voice, Majella said she'd had a dream that she would sing for me.

'Well, now's your chance,' I joked.

Majella didn't think twice about it as she launched into the classic ballad 'She Moved Through the Fair'.

There was a real spark between us that night, and before we parted we made arrangements to meet up again.

Majella said later that she never thought about us becoming a couple because she didn't think that was on the agenda. She felt I wouldn't be interested in 'someone who was going through a divorce and had two children'.

We did embark on a relationship and, when I realised that it was a serious one, I did have second thoughts. Because of my religion, the fact that Majella was previously married gave me cold feet. I also had to consider that young children were involved, as Majella was mum to daughter Siobhan and son Michael, so I was getting involved in the lives of a lot of other people.

However, thank God I had the good sense not to pass up on the chance of happiness in life with Majella. We did part for a time, but remained friends. Then I realised that I was missing Majella when she wasn't around. Love ultimately conquered all the obstacles, and in April 2001 we reunited. I told Majella that I loved her and wanted to spend the rest of my life with her. Luckily, she wanted me as well.

We went public with our relationship on the night of my 40th birthday, 12 December 2001, at a Romanian orphanage charity function I was hosting in Birmingham. And the following Christmas morning I sprung a surprise proposal of marriage on Majella.

Majella was in Donegal for Christmas that year, and Siobhan and Michael were there too. That was our first Christmas together. All of my family came to us for dinner.

At one stage I suggested that Majella should go up to the room and phone her mother and father in Tenerife. Eventually she did slip away to call her parents. I then joined her and when Majella was on to her mother I took the phone and said: 'Now Marion, I have a wee bit of business to do with your daughter. I have to ask her will she marry me!'

Then I put on my song 'Save A Little Lovin'', which was one of Majella's favourites, and produced a ring from my pocket. As I placed the ring on her finger she began to cry and then Marion was crying at the other end of the phone.

When we went downstairs and told all my family, several of them them starting crying, so it was a real royal Irish event with everybody crying.

We got married in my local village church in Kincasslagh the following 4 November. That was a dream come true for me, to wed in the church where I had made my first communion and confimation and where I sang in the choir. And it was a beautiful ceremony when the bride-to-be eventually arrived.

Through no fault of her own, Majella kept me and all 530 of our guests waiting for what seemed like an eternity. It transpired that she was trapped in the wedding car after the electric gates at our home developed a problem and couldn't be opened. The issue was eventually resolved by an expert who was summoned to the scene to avert a catastrophe. There's never a dull moment in my life.

When she eventually glided up the aisle and joined me at the altar, Majella looked every inch a princess in her beautiful pearl-encrusted wedding dress, tiara and flowing veil. During communion I told Majella that I needed a quick loo break. I insisted that I had to go, so she relented and said, 'Don't be long.' Guests in the church were still filing up the aisle to receive communion.

Eventually there was no one left for communion … and there was still an empty seat beside Majella. She looked around slightly embarrassed, and our priest, Fr Brian D'Arcy, looked down and shrugged his shoulders. I'm sure poor Majella was mortified in her seat at this stage.

Then the singing began, and my voice echoed around the church with the opening line, 'You by my side …' I got a side view of Majella and she was totally overcome with emotion. This was my surprise, singing for my bride in church on our wedding day. And Fr Brian had been in on it!

Bonfires greeted the wedding cavalcade along the country roads that evening on our way to the wedding reception at the Holiday Inn in Letterkenny.

In my wedding speech that day I addressed Majella's parents, saying: 'Little did I think when I started gong down to Tom and Marion in their bar that one day I would end up marrying their daughter. I found them to be really genuine. They never wanted me there because I was a singer: they wanted me there because I think they like me. And that's why I went down to them, because I liked them.

'I found that Tom was a great character and a wonderful man and that Marion is one of the few people who can be called a lady in this world.'

I thanked my own family, starting with my siblings, John, Margaret, Kathleen and James, saying: 'All of them in their own way have been so good to me. Kathleen has been like a mother to me and Margaret gave me the opportunity to start my career.'

Then I paid tribute to my mother, Julia, saying: 'I was six when my father died and from then on she has been everything to me. She never let me feel that I needed anything I couldn't get. She gave me security. She gave me love. She gave me encouragement to sing, even at the Burtonport Festival when I was young. "Go over there and enter the talent show," she'd say. I never won, but sure what did they know?', I laughed.

'When I stared singing, it was never ever going to be a part of my plan to get success for being anything other than what I was. My mother was my mother and I was always going to tell the world about how wonderful she was and she will always be that same peson, that wonderful woman who was such an influence in our lives.'

Turning to my bride, Majella, I told the guests how beautiful she was to me when I first caught a glimpse of her in the church that morning. Then I pointed out: 'I know it's not easy for her coming into my world. And I know that there will be times when it's not going to be easy in the future to stay in this world that we're going to live in. But I know together we're a wonderful team. We're great friends. I know she loves me and I love her. So thank you, Majella, for consenting to spend the rest of your life with me.'

I had some personal words also for Siobhan and Michael, saying: 'Everybody is lucky when they get married that they marry someone they want to be with. Well, I think I'm extra lucky because Majella has brought with her Siobhan and Michael. They have accepted me more than I think anybody could be accepted. And I just love it when they come home from school to be with us. I know I can say this, and Majella will back me up, they have a wonderful dad and I will never be anything in their lives compared to him. But I will be the most wonderful friend that you'll ever meet and that's all I want to be.'

In my wedding speech I also remembered the people from the orphanage in Romania, my children, who had become such a wonderful part of my life.

***

Today, in 2017, I can look back and honestly say that meeting Majella was the cream of my personal life. It's the best thing that ever happened to me. It allowed me to have a life.

Up to the time I got married I considered that I had a grand life and I really did enjoy everything, but now that I have this life I realise there was so much that I was missing out on.

I had a wonderful life based around the stage and performing and everything else that I did as an entertainer, but now I'm able to enjoy my off-time as well.

When I look back on the days before I married, I could never say that I was lonely. I didn't have any sense that I was missing out an anything in life. But when I met Majella and our relationship developed, I realised that there is so much more to life and it's wonderful to have someone to share it with. We are very suited, the two of us. We share the same interests. It also helps that Majella understands what I do in my work. She has bought the whole package and I've bought hers too. We all have packages, I suppose.

We are good together and we get on really well. Of course, we have our moments when we disagree over things, but we wouldn't be normal if we didn't. Whatever problems arise, we work them out. We have a great line of communication between us, which I think is important in any marriage.

Marriage happened at the right time in my career. It was so much easier for us because we have a lovely life. Majella's childen were almost grown up, so we were free to do what we liked for the most part. We didn't have the pressures that young married people experience.

Even though I had been a bachelor up to the age of forty, I easily adjusted to sharing my life with Majella. I had been used to my own ways and being able to do anything at the drop of a hat without having to take another person into account, but very quickly I got used to having to think about somebody else. Marriage has fulfilled my life more than I could have hoped for. When you meet someone that you are just at one with, it's a great thing. Before I met Majella I couldn't have imagined how good it could be. Now I think it's a pity that anybody misses out on meeting that special person.

CHAPTER 16

CLIFF RICHARD
AND FRIENDS

Standing on stage in Kincasslagh at the showpiece night of the annual festival in October 2003, I suddenly went into shock when I heard a familiar voice singing: 'Got myself a crying, talking, sleeping, walking, living doll ...'

Then I shook myself out of it as I heard a burst of applause and wild cheering from the 1000-strong audience. I know a man is not supposed to cry over another man, but this was my idol, a living legend, singing on my home stage.

Cliff Richard singing in my native Kincasslagh! I could hardly believe it.

Up to this moment, this feature of the Donegal Shore Festival of Kincasslagh had been known as 'the belle of the ball', where the organisers found me a surprise celebrity belle for the night. Previously they had included the country superstar Loretta Lynn, as I recounted earlier. Liz Dawn, who played Vera Duckworth in *Coronation Street*, was the guest on another occasion, as were my friends, TV presenter Gloria Hunniford and Ireland's first Eurovision Song Contest winner Dana.

But in 2003 I was married to Majella, so the belle went out the window as my new status came in, and the festival organisers replaced her with a special guest.

And, for me, there is nobody more special than Cliff Richard.

Cliff has always been to me what Elvis Presley is to other music fans. He's my favourite male singer and a total inspiration.

I will never forget our night in Kincasslagh. As I told the audience that night, 'You know how much I admire Cliff Richard. This is just unbelievable.'

Then I watched as Cliff sang 'Lucky Lips', 'Travelling Light' and 'Congratulations' before I joined him for a duet on 'All Shook Up'.

And the Elvis song summed up my physical and mental state in that moment.

Cliff stayed at our home on that visit to Kincasslagh for the festival, and that time we spent together solidified our friendship.

***

Just like Loretta Lynn, Cliff didn't disappoint me in person when I first got the opportunity to meet him many years earlier. I had always admired Cliff as a performer and as a person before I got to know him. Songs such as 'Lucky Lips' and 'Living Doll' first connected me to his music. And today one of my favourite songs of all time is his 1976 hit, 'Miss You Nights'.

I first met Cliff at shows, and then one night I went to see his performance in *Heathcliff* at the Edinburgh Playhouse Theatre. Afterwards, we went out to dinner with some friends and I found him a very easy person to be around. Of course, what we had in common was singing and performing in shows, so we chatted about all of that. He was interested in my work and was quite aware of what I was doing in my career at the time.

Cliff was the person I thought he would be before I got to know him. He's a lovely man, and my admiration for him has only been enhanced over the years the more I got to know him. There are so many people who are fans of Cliff yet never get the chance to meet him, so I feel very privileged that we have become pals.

When someone is your idol or your inspiration you put them on a pedestal, but I feel very comfortable around Cliff now. I'm not unnerved meeting him, as I would have been in the beginning. When I go to Cliff's shows these days I go as a fan, but I go backstage as a friend.

Cliff is also very fond of Majella, and he introduced us to his circle of friends, who included the late Cilla Black. We spent time with Cliff and Cilla in Barbados. Gloria Hunniford is another close friend of Cliff and we've all gone on holiday cruises together.

In 2006, Cliff did me the honour of inviting me to do a duet with him on a new album. We recorded The Carpenters' song 'Yesterday Once More'. Other guests on the album included Olivia Newton-John, Phil Everly, Barry Gibb and Dionne Warwick. Cliff had the pick of anybody he wanted, so obviously I was thrilled when he included me among them.

Later I got to sing with him at The Point in Dublin, so that was a very special moment for me. Long before I got to know Cliff or even performed there myself, I went to see his concert at The Point. At that moment I considered The Point to be way out of my league as a venue that I could fill. Somebody asked me that night at Cliff's concert, 'When are you going to play here?' I just laughed because I never had a notion of doing that. And then I did play The Point. And then I was invited on to Cliff's show there as a friend … Well, it just goes to show that you never know how life is going to turn out for you!

***

Sadly, Cilla died in 2015 after a fall in her Spanish home, and it was a terrible shock for her family, friends and legion of devoted fans when the news came through. Cilla was a much-loved entertainer who had connected with so many people through the decades.

Cliff and Cilla were particularly close friends, and he was devastated when he heard the news of her sudden passing. They first met on her TV show *Cilla*, but he says their close friendship really developed when they became neighbours on Barbados.

Cilla couldn't drive, so Cliff became her chauffeur. 'But I refused to wear the cap,' he joked.

I first met Cilla when I appeared on her TV show *Surprise Surprise*. I was on that show a few times, and later I got to know Cilla socially through Cliff. We were all on cruises together, as I mentioned, and we were dinner guests at her home on Barbados. One evening when we went around for dinner, Cilla opened the door with a glass of bubbly in her hand.

'Come in darlings, I'm on a Champagne diet,' Cilla laughed, flashing that gorgeous, big, toothy smile that we all loved.

Then she added: 'I've lost three days already!'

She was such a great character.

***

Cliff has often spoken of how his strong faith helped him to cope with the challenges of life.

I also consider myself fortunate to have a strong faith and a belief in God, and it has helped me through some trying times in my life. I pray every day, although it's talking to God rather than reciting formal prayers. I like to go to Mass and I get a good feeling and great comfort and strength from doing that.

In 2002 on a pilgrimage to Medjugorje in southern Bosnia and Herzegovina, where the Blessed Virgin Mary appeared to six young visionaries in June 1981, I had a strange experience when two songs came to me.

Shortly before that, my friend Marc Roberts had encouraged me to learn the craft of songwriting, which I did under his guidance. Marc is a popular and successful Irish singer and songwriter who represented Ireland in the 1997 Eurovision Song Contest with a John Farry song called 'Mysterious Woman'. He finished in second place that year behind the UK entry, 'Love Shine a Light', sung by Katrina and The Waves.

Marc and I would go on to co-write several songs, including one called 'Crush on You' which was a Top 10 hit in the British pop charts.

On my first day in Medjugorje I climbed the Hill of Apparitions at Podbrdo. This was the place where Our Lady first appeared to all of the children. While I was there my head was suddenly filled with words, and in a blank page of a prayer book I jotted them down. They turned out to be the first verse of a hymn I would later complete, called 'Sweet Queen of Peace'.

Another evening I climbed Cross Mountain, where the pilgrims do the Stations of the Cross along the way, and it was there that the words of the second verse came to me. It goes:

> She tells us to reach out to one another
> To never turn our back on those in need
> And when our world is dark and full of worry
> She'll hurry to our aid and intercede
> I know she'll never leave us or forsake us
> And from our side she never will be far
> And with her son she will protect and keep us
> Sweet Queen of Peace of Medjugorje.

My visit to Medjugorje was an incredible experience. I was there with one of the visionaries one evening when Our Lady appeared to her. I was close by and I could see the woman talking and smiling and listening, although you couldn't hear the words she was speaking. It was a very special moment and I had butterflies in my stomach as I realised what was happening.

I too believe that I was in the presence of Our Lady that evening.

CHAPTER 17

ROYAL TIMES

Prince Charles glided into the room, looking very smart in a dark suit, smiling broadly and speaking in a quiet tone to the people in his company.

Surrounded by my family, I was slightly nervous as I waited my turn to meet the Prince. To my delight, I was about to be presented with an honorary MBE, which had been awarded by Queen Elizabeth in her 2001 New Year's Honours list.

We were all gathered in the British Ambassador's residence in Dublin for the special occasion: my mother, Julia, fiancée Majella, sister Margaret (Margo), brother John, manager Sean Reilly, and friends Josephine Burke and Evelyn Sheehan.

I had never met Prince Charles, but his grandmother was a fan of my music. I know this because Charles and I had a mutual friend called Derek Hill, who was a celebrated artist living in Donegal. Derek was also a great friend of the Queen Mother and had introduced her to my music. Occasionally he would give Prince Charles a new album of mine to pass on to his grandmother.

After I performed at a BBC *Songs of Praise* concert in the Millennium Stadium, Cardiff, in 2000 with many entertainers, including Cliff and Andrew Lloyd Webber, Derek told me that Charles had asked him, 'Isn't that the chap whose music you gave me for my grandmother?'

So that day at the MBE presentation in Dublin I had the comfort of knowing that at least Prince Charles had an awareness of what I do in life.

Watching the Prince move around the room, I was delighted that my mother had lived to see this moment. To have Mother there on the special day meant the world to me. However, it also put me on edge.

My mother, you see, absolutely idolised Princess Diana. She kept Diana scrapbooks with cuttings from newspapers and magazines that had stories and photographs of the Princess through the years. I wasn't sure how she felt about Prince Charles, but I had her warned to be on her best behaviour. I had said to her, 'Now, Mother, don't you be saying anything.'

My mother, you see, was a straight-talking woman.

I was thinking back to the time she met Loretta Lynn's husband, Doolittle, as I have mentioned already. Mother had been to see *Coal Miner's Daughter*, a movie based on Loretta's life. Doolittle didn't come out of that film looking too good – he was portrayed as a husband who had given Loretta a hard time. When my mother met Doolittle at the TV studios in Dublin the time Loretta appeared on my show, she said to him in a sharp tone, 'You were a right boyo!' She said nothing more, but she didn't need to.

By the horrified look on his face it was obvious that Doolittle understood what hadn't been said.

I was mortified!

So here I am with Prince Charles about to approach me and I'm thinking, 'Mother, please be on your best behaviour or he won't give me the MBE!' To my relief, she couldn't have given him a warmer reception. And he was lovely to my mother, carrying on a very normal conversation. We were all very impressed by Prince Charles and his common touch.

Then came the formal presentation and some of the reasons for it. The citation referred to my contribution to the music industry and my charity work. My mother's face couldn't hide the pride she was feeling. And for me, that was the best part of receiving an MBE.

As my mother chatted with Prince Charles I heard her tell him, 'I sent a card to your two boys when Diana died.'

'That was very nice of you,' Charles replied.

***

Going back, I will never forget the moment I was told that Diana, Princess of Wales, was in a critical condition after a car crash in Paris on 31 August 1997.

I was away in America at the time, and a friend from home called me shortly after hearing the news. We turned on the TV and it was all over the news. It had just been confirmed that Diana's boyfriend Dodi Fayed was dead.

I was staying with an Irish priest from home called Fr Michael Cannon, and I said to him, 'This will finish Diana now.' She'd had so much trauma in her life and I felt that Dodi's death would push her over the edge.

Above: Thousands for tea! The scene outside my home in Kincasslagh on a summer's day in 1992 when three thousand people turned up to meet me. **Below:** Watching the crowds arrive with my late mother Julia and sister Margaret (Margo).

Above: At home with the clan. In the back row are my nephew John Francis, brother-in-law John Doogan, niece Patricia, myself, my sister-in-law Brigid, brother John and nephew Frankie. In the front are my sister Kathleen, my mother, my nephew Daniel, my sister Margaret (Margo), niece Fiona and nephew Joey.

Right: Singing at midnight mass at Christmas in our local church.

Keeping me in order on tour in the early days: Joe Collum (driver and organiser), Loretta Flynn (fan club secretary) and Jim Rosie (compère).

My band in 1992: Ray McLoughlin, John Staunton, Billy Condon, me, Tony Murray and Richard Nelson. Front: Billy Burgoyne and Ronnie Kennedy.

Over six thousand people turned up for my Welcome Back show at Dublin's Point Theatre in July 1992. It was a night to remember.

Above left: A royal occasion: Prince Charles presents me with an honorary MBE in 2001 at the British Ambassador's residence in Dublin.

Above: The happy couple! Majella and me on our wedding day, 4 November 2002, in Kincasslagh.

Left: Recording the live album *Songs of Faith* in The Helix theatre, Dublin, in 2003.

Opposite: Since 2015, Majella and I have had great fun travelling around Ireland for the UTV Ireland and RTÉ series *Daniel and Majella's B&B Road Trip*.

One of the biggest challenges of my career was competing on the
Strictly Come Dancing BBC TV show in the UK. My professional partner
Kristina Rihanoff did her best to make me look good!

In January 2016 we embarked on the holiday of a lifetime: a four-month luxury cruise around the world. Places we visited include Japan, Vietnam, French Polynesia and Phuket Island.

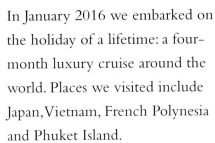

Above: Here I am with my former manager, Sean Reilly, my current manager, Kieran Cavanagh, and Eddie Rowley, co-author of this book and showbiz editor at the *Sunday World*.

There was no update on Diana's condition when we retired to bed. It was the following morning when I learned the awful news. Father Michael knocked on my bedroom door, came into the room and said, 'Diana didn't make it.'

I hadn't been expecting to hear that she had died and I actually went into a state of shock. I couldn't even lift my head off the pillow. It was just terrible to think that someone as beautiful and vibrant as Princess Di could be cut down in her prime and so quickly.

The following year, 1998, when I was in Paris doing a photo shoot for my *Love Songs* album, I had the opportunity to pay my respects to Diana by laying a bouquet of flowers near the tunnel under the Place de L'Alma where she died.

In my mind, I still found it difficult to accept that Diana was no longer with us.

***

That 1998 trip to Paris to shoot a series of photographs for *Love Songs* turned out to be great fun. Mick McDonagh, my creative consultant going back to my first album, set it all up. However, being a rugby fan, he had missed the fact that France was then hosting the (soccer) World Cup and the streets were choc-a-bloc with fans.

The day after our arrival we were all set up taking photographs outside one of the busy cafés when a gang of guys in tartan started serenading me with the Irish ballad 'Danny Boy'.

'There's only one thing I'm going to do now, Mick,' I said, brushing aside the camera.

'What's that Daniel?' he asked, looking alarmed.

'I'm going over to join those boys!'

In situations like that, I'm a firm believer in stepping up to the mark and introducing yourself to strangers so that they can get to know you and then decide whether or not they like you.

So over I went and asked: 'How are youse doin'?'

And before I knew it guys in kilts were handing me mobile phones to talk to their loved ones back in Scotland. I guess they had a few brownie points to build up, so I was good for that.

One fella said to me, 'Och, I'll be all right now that my wife knows I'm with you. She won't be thinkin' I'm in the pub.'

I spoke to wives, mothers-in-law, grandmothers, mothers, sisters, you name it, that day. It was great fun. And we eventually got some photographs too.

***

As the years went on, I never developed a passion for photo and video shoots. The only time I got excited about this process was when it gave me the opportunity to show off some of Ireland's historical and beauty spots.

My 1999 video for *Peaceful Waters* took me on a boat trip from the north to the south of Ireland, taking in historic monuments, castles, stately homes, and quaint little pubs and restaurants along the way.

It was a great chance to explore the history, myths and legends of Ireland. I recall visiting a church around Lough Erne which was the inspiration for a storyline in the film *The Quiet Man*. In that movie a bishop visits a Protestant community where he is planning to close the church because of a fall in numbers. However, the local Catholic priest helps out by getting his people to attend the church, urging them to, 'Cheer like good Protestants!' That story apparently came from the community I visited on my cruise along the waterway.

Peaceful Waters is one of my favourite videos. I love the way it was constructed, the songs, my dialogue and the fact that it's informative.

Sometimes my video shoots caused a stir at the various locations, and one in particular created quite a bit of confusion, as two letters to the *Irish Times* newspaper in June 1996 will tell you.

The first one read:

Sir – Can any of your readers explain why the outlets of the Templecrone Co Operative Society in Kincasslagh and Dungloe are getting ready for Christmas? On June 1st, I was in Donegal, and both shops had full Christmas displays in their windows with seasonal floristry, poinsettia, holly and the like, jolly exhortations to customers to have a happy season and a prosperous New Year, and in the case of Dungloe, a cornucopia of toys, tinsel and bows, with Santa himself beaming from his icy groto.

I know that Christmas starts early every year, but surely this is a record! Yours, etc.,

Margaret McCann

Dunshaughlin

Co Meath

The letter got a reply:

Sir – A Ms McCann (June 15) seeks an explanation as to why shops in

Kincasslagh and Dungloe had full Christmas displays on June 1.

Daniel O'Donnell was simply shooting his Christmas video in Kincasslagh on that day. On closer inspection she would have noticed that the place was also covered with snow!

It's not a record, it's a video.

Yours, etc.,

Paul Buckley

Clare Road

Donegal

Yes, indeed, I did turn Kincasslagh to winter that summer! It was a lot cheaper than travelling to Alaska at that time of the year to do a Christmas video.

A cousin of my mother was home on holiday from Scotland and knew nothing about the video. He scratched his head in disbelief when he entered Danny Minnie's bar and found it all decked out with Christmas decorations … and a fella dressed as Santa sitting in the corner.

An auld fella went in to the local Iggy's pub when the sun was shining on a summer's day, spent several hours, and came out to find the place covered in snow.

I reckon it was enough to make him give up the drink.

One of my favourite Christmas videos is from 1999 and we shot it in The Central Hotel in Dublin, where I had been employed as a dishwasher nineteen years earlier.

It's my favourite for another personal reason, as it features comic Caroline Aherne, aka 'Mrs Merton', the British TV character.

I'd had great fun with Caroline when I appeared on her hilarious TV series *The Mrs Merton Show* in the UK. I have to admit that I had never seen the show before I agreed to be a guest on it. So I was surprised by the reaction when I announced that I was going to be appearing. People wrote and told me that it was very risky doing that show, as 'Mrs Merton' was very irreverent.

Although some people warned that she would tear me to shreds, 'Mrs Merton' was gentle with me. We did have a good laugh on the show, especially when she asked me in the interview if I 'trump'.

I hadn't a clue what she meant and told her: 'I don't know what that means. I really don't know if I do or not.'

So 'Mrs Merton' explained it to me, and I blurted out:

'Oh, you mean farting!'

Well, that got a laugh.

Later I learned that Caroline's grandmother lived in Gort, County Galway, and was a fan of mine. Maybe she had warned her to be nice to me.

Caroline then agreed to appear in a new video for my single, 'A Christmas Kiss', in which she played a battleaxe office manager. I was the post boy, but at Christmas I'm transformed into a rock hunk playing in a band at the office party and 'Mrs Merton' is absolutely besotted, battling through the dancers with mistletoe to plant a big kiss on my lips.

I was absolutely shocked when I heard that Caroline had died from lung cancer at the age of 52 in July 2016. The much-loved actress, who also won numerous awards for the hugely popular British TV sitcom *The Royle Family*, which she co-wrote and starred in as Denise, had been battling the disease for years.

A close friend said that ten days before she died, Caroline was laughing and joking. Although she knew the end was near, she said she had achieved everything that she wanted and was happy.

Still, Caroline is gone too soon.

CHAPTER 18

LIVING THE
NIGHTMARE

I don't think anything prepares you for the word 'cancer' entering your life, or the life of a loved one.

Neither Majella nor myself was expecting to hear that term in July 2013 when we attended a second appointment at the Beacon Hospital in Dublin.

In the lead-up to that moment, Majella had discovered a lump in her breast and phoned her doctor straight away to have it checked out. If there is a problem, the sooner you get a diagnosis, the greater the chance of recovery.

We had been to the Beacon together where the tests were conducted, but then Majella had got a call back. I was in Tenerife when she received this news, and I got the next available flight home, even though Majella insisted that it was unnecessary. She said they wanted to do a more thorough test or something to that effect.

Majella didn't seem to be worried as we drove down from Donegal that day. We certainly weren't expecting the bombshell when we met the consultant at the Beacon Hospital the following day.

I think we both felt a sense of foreboding when we realised that it was Terry, the consultant, who was seeing Majella. It seemed odd that Terry would be there for what Majella had thought was just another test. But when we eventually met him in his office, Terry had Majella's report and he presented it to us in a very formal way, like you would hear evidence given in court. Majella said later that the language Terry used helped her to cope with the message that was being delivered.

Terry read the report: 'You are Majella O'Donnell and you presented yourself to this clinic with a lump in your left breast. You underwent the triple assessment and had a biopsy taken of your breast tissue. The biopsy has shown that there are cancerous cells present in your breast.'

I was holding Majella's hand and at this point we squeezed each other's hand. My emotions were welling up, but I managed to suppress the tears. Majella was very strong, asking what all this meant and what was going to happen next.

She said later that if Terry had told her, 'I'm sorry to tell you Majella that you have cancer,' she might have gone to pieces. But the enormity of the situation didn't really sink in at that moment.

At the end of July, Majella underwent surgery to have the lump removed. However, when she returned to hospital and was told that the next stage of the treatment involved chemotherapy, it finally registered with her that she was fighting cancer. She said the introduction of chemotherapy shocked her more than being told she had cancer. It really frightened her, knowing there are side-effects: sickness, being debilitated and losing her hair.

Then somewhere along the way Majella had a brainwave that she would turn this negative situation into a positive by raising funds to support cancer sufferers. Majella has been through many adversities in her life and there is no doubt that she is a fighter. She has spoken openly about her battle with depression and how she copes with that. Majella is a remarkable woman who confronts head-on the challenges of life, but even I wasn't prepared for what she did next.

Knowing that she was going to lose her hair as a result of the chemo-therapy treatment, Majella decided to have her head shaved live on television to raise money for charity and to create an awareness of breast cancer.

At this stage I was away on tour in America at the insistence of Majella. My initial reaction when she was diagnosed with cancer was to cancel everything to be with her. But she insisted that life should go on as normal. Majella also pointed out that there wasn't an awful lot I could do for her. She said it was something she had to go through herself, and knowing she had my support was all that mattered: whether I was in Timbuktu or beside her, I was equally beneficial to her. However, I was still feeling awful being so far away.

Majella rang me in the States and told me what she was then planning – having her head shaved for charity live on *The Late Late Show*, Ireland's biggest TV chat show, hosted by Ryan Tubridy. I was naturally taken aback by such a brave move, but I was fully supportive. The only issue I had was Majella's financial expectation of €10,000. I felt she should set a target of at least €100,000. With Irish people struggling through the worst recession in living memory at the time, Majella felt that that was an unrealistic figure. So she compromised and set a target of €50,000.

The Late Late Show team and presenter Ryan Tubridy were very supportive of Majella. Even at the final hour they gave her the opportunity to change her mind. But Majella was adamant that she would do the job. Once she has set her mind to something, she is the type of person who will see it through to fruition. She really is a very strong, determined lady, and in this case she needed to summon up every ounce of courage to do what she ultimately did. In front of a TV studio audience and with hundreds of thousands of viewers watching the live broadcast, Majella went through the process of having her head shaved until she was completely bald.

'This is a challenge that I have been able to turn into a positive, as I do with most adversities in my life,' she said in an interview with the *Sunday World* newspaper. 'It's the type of person I am. I've had my challenges with my first marriage breaking up and my depression, and now I have my challenge with cancer. But other people have challenges too and there are many who have far heavier crosses to bear. All these crosses help you to be a stronger person. And my previous crosses have helped me to be as strong as I am for this challenge. I'm very grateful for that.'

Majella's target of raising €10,000 for the cancer charity was way off the mark. As it turned out, my own target of €100,000 was also a drop in the ocean compared to the amount of money Majella's head-shave eventually raised. There was an incredible outpouring of support from the Irish public. Majella received an avalanche of beautiful, heart-warming messages on social media. And she was astonished, as was I, when more than €700,000 was ultimately donated to the charity by the people of Ireland.

Doing that charity drive was actually very beneficial to Majella as well. She said that on days when she was going through a really difficult time she would think about the money that was raised and the good it was doing. The cash was for the support of the ordinary, everyday person. There were people going through similar treatment who couldn't afford a wig, or who needed support with household bills because they couldn't work and didn't have an income, or people who needed counselling and transport ... all of the practical day-to-day stuff.

Majella said she felt very fortunate that she didn't have to worry about the financial side of things.

'The least I can do is sit and be humiliated in front of the nation as I go bald,' she joked.

At the end of her chemo, Majella wanted to be certain that the cancer was gone from her body, so she asked to have a double mastectomy and that surgery was carried out in February 2014, followed by reconstruction. Thankfully, all of that went well. Even though Majella had to go through the treatment and the surgery and everything that goes with it, she realises she is very fortunate that her cancer was such an early diagnosis. And we have every faith that that's the end of it.

All along the way we held on to the positives in it. Once the bad word came, the diagnosis, everything else that we were getting back was positive. You thrive on the good results that you get from there on.

***

Shortly after Majella began her chemotherapy treatment she received a phone call, on 12 October 2013, that left her completely heartbroken. Her father, Tom, was in a critical condition in a Tenerife hospital after suffering a suspected brain haemhorrage. Majella's mother, Marion, who was looking after her at the time in Ireland, was asleep in bed at our Dublin apartment when the devastating call came through. It was Majella who had to wake her with the awful news. That is a terrible moment she will never forget.

Tom was on a life-support machine, and it was a harrowing ordeal for all the members of his loving family to see him in that state. Several days later the decision was taken to take Tom off life support after tests revealed that he had no brain activity whatsoever. And then he slowly slipped away.

Tom was a wonderful character and he and I were great friends. We went back a long way, as I had known Tom and Marion before I met Majella. After we married and bought our villa in the hills of Tenerife, Tom was always there to look after it. Whenever there was any DIY or gardening to be done, Tom was the man who did it. I've never mastered DIY and not even trips to Knock, Lourdes and Medjugorje could fix that. So, if there was a problem, Tom would get the call.

He was full of wit and wisdom. He was very entertaining and always great company to be with. He loved people and was the life and soul of the party wherever a crowd had gathered.

I remember him making a lovely father-of-the-bride speech on our wedding day and warmly welcoming me into the Roche family, although I was well ensconced by then. Tom recalled how he and Marion had known me for eight years, adding that it was 'long before Majella met him'. He went on to say how my joining the Roche family just seemed like a progresssion of our friendship over all the years.

Then my new father-in-law paid me a lovely compliment when he added that he and Marion were so happy for their daughter, Majella, 'to meet such a wonderful person'.

I have such fond memories of Tom, including all the times we played cards together, which was another thing Tom, Marion and I had in common.

Majella's treatment was very tough, but her father losing his life in the middle of it was an awful lot of sorrow and pain for her to have to deal with at the same time.

***

The journey of life takes many twists and turns, and is marked by joy and sadness, love and loss. And no matter what your status, there is no escape from the heartache and trauma that comes knocking.

In May 2014 it would be my turn to start the journey into bereavement when my beloved mother, Julia, died at the age of ninety-four.

CHAPTER 19

QUEEN OF OUR HOME

I t hardly needs to be stated that it's not easy to let your mother go, to see her life ebb away. We selfishly want to keep the people we love in our lives forever, but God ultimately calls all of us. And in my mother's case there was the consolation of knowing that she had been spared suffering.

Up to the moment of her passing on Sunday, 18 May 2014, my mother's memory was still razor sharp. We were asking her questions and she was able to tell us the answers. She had received prayer beads from the Pope and we asked her in the hospital where she kept them in the family home, as we wanted her to have them with her when she died. And Mam was able to describe to us where they could be found, so there was nothing wrong with her memory.

However, in her last year I did feel that her time was near. It's not that she was sick, but I could see that she was tired. While her mind was as alert as ever, her body just wore out. She literally died of old age.

Thankfully, as we said our goodbyes to Mam in the hospital in Dungloe that Sunday in May, there were no regrets. Throughout her life, Mam had done her best for her family, and in return she got buckets of love from all of us. She dedicated her life to her children, grandchildren and great grand-childen – and in return she was surrounded by love to the end.

Although Mam grew up in primitive times on the island of Owey, she went on to make her mark in the world, connecting with people from all walks of life. For me, the most rewarding aspect of my singing career was the fact that I was able to include my mother, open up doors for her and give her a platform in life. And, boy, did she enjoy that platform. I always made a point of putting the spotlight on her at my concerts and then everyone in every hall and arena got Mam's royal wave. She was our Queen Mother.

When she penned her own life story, Mam said: 'For all the downs that I've had with my husband not being around, and the loneliness I've experienced as a widow, there have been more ups. I know in my heart and soul that God has been more than good to me and that I've been more fortunate than most.

'I've seen the world and met all kinds of wonderful people. There's hardly a day goes by that the postman doesn't drop cards or letters through my door from some of Daniel's fans.

'I love the fact that at my age I still have a connection with so many people. It keeps me going. I am blessed that I'm not hidden away and forgotten. I am still getting great enjoyment out of life through Daniel and all the rest of my lovely family.'

Looking back, it was my mother who first encouraged me to get up on stage when I was a child. She always wanted me to sing. Whenever there was an opportunity to do so she would say, 'You get up now, go on,' from the time I was very small. She had me singing anywhere and everywhere. I suppose that helped to build my confidence to do it. Every little step I took back then was a step towards what would ultimately become my career. And she obviously did the same with my sister Margaret.

Mam brought me around to different places to sing in local bars and hotels from the age of eight or nine upwards. It's not that she was preparing me for a career; she just wanted me to sing. Maybe it was all for fun, or it could have been Mam's way of helping me to develop as a child.

She was asked in an interview one time how she felt about me giving up college to sing. Her response was that she didn't want to stop me doing what I wanted to do, or influence me to take another path, for fear it wouldn't work out for me. She wouldn't have wanted to have that on her conscience, so she left it up to me to follow my instinct.

My mother let me fly to do what I wanted, and she loved the career Margaret and myself had in music. She loved every aspect of the music business, loved being a part of it and being at all the major events. She was made for it really.

That's how all the people got to know her. She loved people and maybe that's where I got my love of people. She loved people around her, talking to her, and she would be in her element. And she loved being made a fuss of.

I do think that if my mother had been born later and given the opportunities, she would have had a terrific career of her own. She was very clever and when she'd write letters they were so well composed. I do think she would have been a career woman of some sort.

We were discussing this after she died and my brother John said, 'I think she would have been a barrister, or she might have been running the country now.' And you know, he's right.

Mam loved writing letters and after she died we were flabbergasted at the discoveries we made in her correspondence, of the people she had written to and the responses she had received. We didn't know or realise some of the things she did.

There was a letter written on behalf of Princes William and Harry thanking Mam for the letter she had sent to them after their mother had died in the Paris car crash. On the tenth anniversary of Diana's death there was a concert celebrating her life, and Mam again wrote to her two sons and sent them pictures of their mother, which was acknowledged in a letter back to her.

Nothing dazzled my mother: she was the same with neighbours as she was with famous people. I might consider writing to William or Harry, but then I'd think, 'Sure what would I be doing that for?' But Mam thought her letter was as important to them as any other letter they were going to get. A lot of people said to me since she died that they too received letters from my mother when they suffered bereavements. They were so touched that she took the time to sit down and write a letter to them. I don't want to canonise her, but she really was something else.

Another of my mother's favourite pastimes was knitting, and she would knit for family and friends to pass the time. She also knitted gloves and socks that she sent to dignitaries. Pope Benedict and Pope Francis, and Queen Elizabeth, received gifts of gloves from her. A passionate Celtic

FC supporter, she sent their then manager, Neil Lennon, a pair of gloves and she was delighted when she spotted him on TV wearing them at a match. Other well-known people who received gloves from her included former Donegal football manager Jim McGuinness, Irish TV personality Daithi O'Shea and the then American President Barack Obama and his wife, Michelle.

It delighted my mother greatly when she received letters of thanks from all these dignitaries. I dread to think what the outcome would have been had they not replied. Mind you, a few of them took their time in replying and this did not go down well with Mam.

Even though I could see that Mam's time on earth was getting shorter and I suspected that 2014 was going to be her final year, I still can't believe how unprepared I was for the moment when she did die. We were all trying to console ourselves with the fact that she was a great age and that we were lucky to have had her in our lives, but it didn't stop the pain. The queen of our house was gone.

There were moments when I was very composed, and one of those times was in the hospital when she died. In that moment I decided to sing, 'My Lovely Island Home', which Mam had written in the 1970s about her beloved Owey Island.

By the middle of the 1970s there were only three families still living on Owey. They would spend the winters on the mainland, and return to their Owey homes for the summer. However, the day came when they all opted to live full-time on the mainland, where they had all of the modern conveniences. And when the last family left, Mam said it was one of the saddest days of her life. She loved Owey like a family member. Mam cried in our home that day thinking about the island being deserted. Mammy's life on the island had been really hard, but it was the life of all of that generation. When she spoke about her early life it was never with a sense of suffering; it was always with a sense of joy and longing for it because she felt the island was so beautiful.

Thinking about Owey that day, Mam realised that nothing had ever been written about the island and its history and traditions. And in that hour she was inspired to sit down and pen a poem about the island of her birth:

MY LOVELY ISLAND HOME
As I sit here sadly thinking how the years go swiftly past
My thoughts go back to my childhood day when I was but a lass
And we a happy family gathered round our turf fire bright
And the fairytales our parents told on the cold dark wintry nights

My brothers they are married now with families of their own
My sister lives in the USA in her grand Long Island home
She pays a visit now and then to greet us one and all
Then our thoughts go back to those happy times in our home in Donegal

My island home lies empty now, the clock hangs on the wall
The fireside chair it still sits there, there's a padlock on the door
The raging seas and the wintry winds and the seagulls wearily cry
But no fire burns bright in our hearth tonight
As it did in days gone by

So fare thee well my island home, where I spent many happy days
And fare thee well to my friends so dear, who have crossed the ocean waves

May God protect and guide you all, wherever you may roam

For Owey was like Heaven to us in our happy island home.

In 2006, when I was working on an album of my own songs, I put some music to Mam's poem and I recorded it. That is now one of the songs on my album *Until the Next Time*. It is a song that has great significance for me and our family and the people who came from Owey.

Mam was so proud that she had written that song and, as I have mentioned, I sang 'My Lovely Island Home' at her hospital bedside after she passed away. She was no distance away at the time because she had literally died five minutes earlier, so her spirit was not far from her body. Mam was one of those lucky people in life who derived such joy and goodness and well-being from music and song. When I visited her in the hospital before she died, there was another wee woman in her room and she was ninety-seven years old.

'You should hear this woman sing,' Mam said to me.

Then she persuaded the wee woman to sing a beautiful old song.

'Now,' said Mam, 'what do you think of that!'

And, of course, she then insisted that I should sing a song in return.

Mam just loved that.

***

My mother always had her own distinctive style with her dresses and cardigans. She took great pride in her appearance and had a fascination for handbags. After she died we got Mam's hair done, as she would have liked, and her make-up. When I saw her in the coffin in the funeral home, I couldn't believe how nice she looked. She was so like herself in life.

Then we took her back to the family home where she had reigned as our queen through all of our lives. As we stood around her in the room feeling so sorry for our loss, it suddenly struck me how my mother must have felt almost forty-six years previously when our father died and she was left alone with a family of five: the eldest, John, being just nineteen years old at the time. What must that have been like, what step was she going to take forward in really hard times and not knowing where the money would come from? It must have been frightening for her, but, as I said, she was a very strong woman, very resilient.

Margaret and I had decided that we wouldn't sing at the funeral Mass in the church, as emotionally we just wouldn't have been able to do that. Mam had always wanted 'Will the Circle Be Unbroken?' to be sung when she died. We did sing it for Mam in her home, and then we sang 'My Lovely Island Home' again. It seemed the right thing to do because Mammy loved the singing.

Hundreds of people turned out to give Mam a right royal send-off at her funeral in our local St Mary's Church, Kincasslagh. Eleven priests concelebrated the mass, and she would have been delighted with that. The music in the church would also have been to her liking. I always feel that weddings and funerals should have religious songs, and that's what we had for my mother's funeral. Mary Duff was the singer and she sang beautifully.

At my mother's request, the chief celebrant was Fr Brian Logue, who came home from Scotland for the funeral. Fr Logue is originally from Kincasslagh and he had celebrated the mass at my father's funeral in the same church almost forty-six years previously.

In his eulogy, Fr Logue said: 'Julia was a wonderful mother. The children were also blessed, as I would know, with a wonderful father, Francie. I have no doubt now that he and Julia are together again in the Kingdom of God.'

He went on: 'She was a gifted and talented person. She was very well known for her knitting; she knitted for the Pope, she knitted for the Queen and she received thank-you letters from both of them.'

Fr Logue then remarked: 'I cannot count the number of clerical black socks she knitted for me.' It was a light-hearted moment that made us all laugh.

Referring to Mam's talent for writing poetry and songs, he said: 'When Daniel was nine years old he was at our home in Kincasslagh and he offered to sing a song for us. It was called "There's a Shop at the Corner Called Logues"'. My father's shop. It was the first ever recorded song by Daniel. We still have the tape, the very first recording. And the "studio" it was recorded in was Logues' kitchen!'

Remarking on the number of priests concelebrating the Mass, Fr Logue recalled: 'My own mother after every funeral used to measure the person by the number of priests who were there. If there were a good few she would be pleased. I hope today then that Julia would be pleased because all the priests here are friends.'

Mam's final resting place was Belcruit Cemetery, where she was buried alongside the husband she had adored, my father Francie. Mam was interred wearing her wedding ring. She had given instructions that she wanted the wedding ring left on her finger where my father had placed it.

At the graveside our sister Margaret said a few lovely words. Then she handed me the microphone and said, 'Sing if you want to.' I had no intention of singing, but at that moment I felt very strong. So I sang a song called 'Beyond the Rainbow's End', which I had composed myself, and I was able to finish it without breaking down.

That was a strange moment because when I first wrote and recorded 'Beyond the Rainbow's End', my mother loved it and had asked, 'Will you sing that at my funeral?'

'How could I sing that at your funeral?!' I asked her.

'And why not?' she asked.

'Sure I would be too upset,' I said.

But on the day I did sing the song, and I managed to get through it without crumbling.

So Mam got her wish.

And later I thought that, yes, the sentiments in 'Beyond the Rainbow's End' were so appropriate in the moment:

I have gone from sight, but I am waiting
Waiting just beyond the rainbow's end
I'm happy in this place that I have come to
Because I'm here with my forever friend

Now all your thoughts of me let them be joyful
Of things we've done and happy times we've shared
So don't be sad dear ones because I've left you
Please laugh and talk of me as if I'm there

Just look up in the sky, I am the sunshine
I'm the mist that rises on a summer's morn
I'm the gentle breeze that cools the autumn evening
When the birds sing in the trees, I am their song

This journey I have made, one day you'll make it

You too will be my forever friend

It's then once more that we will be together

I'll meet you just beyond the rainbow's end

It's then once more that we will be together

I'll meet you just beyond the rainbow's end

Yes I'm waiting just beyond the rainbow's end.

CHAPTER 20

TV ROAD TRIPS WITH MAJELLA

In 2015 Majella and I did our first Irish reality TV series together, called *Daniel and Majella's B&B Road Trip*. The huge popularity that the show enjoyed took us completely by surprise.

This was one of the projects I embarked on when I took time off from touring. Initially, Majella and I had a vision of doing a travel show in Ireland to showcase our lovely country and all the wonderful features that it has to offer. My manager, Kieran Cavanagh, took the idea to a production company and they then developed it into what ultimately became a B&B road trip.

It was a very simple format that featured the two of us travelling around Ireland by car and staying at the country's famed bed and breakfast houses with local families.

A camera documented the trip and filmed our conversations and banter in the car as we journeyed through the countryside. In each destination we were given a surprise challenge or activity, most of which took us out of our comfort zones. I have a fear of water, but I had to overcome that phobia when I did adventure sports like kayaking and paddle boarding in Bantry Bay, and we both threw our dignity to the wind when we agreed to engage in a hilarious activity called zorbing.

The show went on to win an Irish Film & Television Award (IFTA) … our very own Oscar!

I think what made it such a big hit with the viewers was the interaction between the pair of us, particularly in the car, and the great characters we encountered in the B&Bs.

The conversations we had in the car were no different to the ones that we have when there are no cameras around. We just said it as it was, for good or bad. Sometimes it's a nippy conversation and sometimes it's a friendly one. That's just the way we roll in real life, as Majella would say.

One journalist asked me what I learned from doing the *B&B Road Trip*, and when I reflected on the question I said it reminded Majella and me just how well we get on as a couple. We are very different in many ways, but also very compatible. Even if we're doing nothing in particular we're very comfortable in each other's company. Majella says I make her laugh and that we're not afraid of upsetting each other. If we have a disagreement I like to talk it out until it's resolved, while Majella will shut down and let it linger. But having lived life, we keep everything in perspective and don't get too hot and bothered about things that are really not all that important at the end of the day.

One of the B&B superstars in the first series was a lady called Anne Sheerin from Tulsk, County Roscommon. Anne happened to be a Daniel fan, and her emotional reaction to my arrival at her beautiful B&B home in that gorgeous part of rural Ireland was just hilarious to watch. It featured in the promotion for the first series and then it went viral on the internet, giving us the perfect launch for our TV career. If it was fictional and we were casting a character, I don't think we could have invented Anne. She was such good fun, and so bubbly and warm.

Next stop was Moy River B&B near Cloonacool, County Sligo, a lovely home-from-home run by a very engaging couple called Pat and Rita McCarrick. The local area is also beautiful, truly a hidden gem.

When the viewing figures for that first episode came in, we couldn't believe the result. More than half a million viewers had tuned in to watch the show. It was the biggest programme on UTV Ireland that year outside of the soaps.

UTV Ireland also pointed out that 'Anne Sheerin from Tulsk, who featured in last night's episode, has become an internet sensation – her reaction to Daniel and Majella arriving at her B&B has reached more than 1.5 million people through UTV Ireland's Facebook page alone and has been shared on all media platforms many, many times.'

There were plenty of laughs along the way, usually at my expense as I looked like a right eejit doing some of the activities. But occasionally I did a bit of leg pulling myself.

In Gort, County Galway, we stayed at Naomh Colman B&B, owned by Josephine Finnegan and her husband Pat. Their B&B is famous for its view of Ireland's tallest round tower and Kilmacduagh monastery, an archaeological treasure that was founded by St Colman.

Josephine had been filmed saying that she doesn't include beans as part of her full Irish breakfast. She insisted that beans at breakfast is an English tradition. And Josephine was adamant that she wouldn't make an exception for anybody, including my good self. Well, you'd think I was after ordering the Crown Jewels to be served up on my plate when I asked for them. Josephine's expression was priceless.

Nevertheless, like a good B&B hostess, she didn't disappoint me.

'You know beans are not part of an Irish breakfast, but seeing it's you …,' she replied.

And so I got my beans!

Pat and his two sons are such avid Liverpool supporters that they have turned Josephine's vegetable patch into their very own Anfield soccer pitch, where Majella and I were challenged to a game of football with local children.

At Carrigaholt in County Clare we booked into the Glencarrig Farmhouse B&B, run by Mary and Luke Aston. It is sitting in a gorgeous setting with magnificent views of the River Shannon and Kerry Mountains. We enjoyed a day of fishing on Luke's boat to catch our own dinner. And that evening we feasted on the fish we landed after they were served up to us at the local Long Dock restaurant, where all of Mary and Luke's children were working.

On our trip through beautiful West Kerry we stopped off at O'Connor's Guesthouse in Cloghane, run by local man Mícheál O'Dowd and his charming American-born wife, Sherry. It is situated on the Wild Atlantic Way and a great place to stop over. Mícheál is a fount of knowledge about the area and county and I'm sure the tourists absolutely love him.

In Bantry, County Cork, we stayed in a B&B called Edencrest, owned and run by a vivacious lady called Josephine Walsh.

As a native of Thurles, County Tipperary, Majella was delighted to see popular local B&B Inch House on our itinerary. Run by John and Norah Egan, it's situated on their farm in Inch, Bouladuff. The house is a beautiful Georgian building which was originally constructed back in 1720. John and Norah have eight children and there are four generations of the family living and working in the house.

The Cut Loose Country Festival was in full swing at Holy Cross when we were down in that neck of the woods. I dropped by to see headline act Nathan Carter wowing the crowds, and he invited me up on stage to join him in a song.

At the Celtic House B&B, situated in the heart of the historic city of Kilkenny, we got a warm welcome from the owners, Angela and John Byrne. Angela is referred to as 'Ireland's Goodwill Ambassador to the World' by Lonely Planet. While staying in the hometown of the GAA, we got to follow in the footsteps of Kilkenny greats with a hurling lesson. Angela, who is a member of the local Soulful Spirit gospel choir, also invited us to enjoy an exclusive performance.

***

Majella and I went tractor racing in Enniskerry, County Wicklow, on the trip. Our B&B stay in 'The Garden of Ireland', as Wicklow is known, was at Coolakay House in Enniskerry, owned by perfect hosts Robert and Yvonne Rowe. The B&B is located on a working farm where sheep farmer Robert also has a museum dedicated to Irish farming through the ages, with some machinery used by his grandparents from times gone by.

In the medieval coastal town of Carlingford, County Louth, we were guests at Shalom B&B, which is overlooked by the beautiful Cooley Mountains on one side and the stunning Mournes on the other. Shalom, which also has incredible views across Carlingford Lough, is the home of Kevin and Jackie Woods.

Kevin, we later discovered, is Ireland's last 'leprechaun whisperer', known locally as Mac Coillte (the son of the woods man).

In 2003, legend has it, Kevin found a leather purse with four coins in it while he was fixing a wall in Carlingford. It also contained a note from a famous Carlingford publican called P.J. O'Hare, who is said to have found a leprechaun hat, tunic, trousers and bones on the mountain over-looking the picturesque town.

Kevin said in a newspaper interview that he first stumbled upon three leprechauns sitting on a rock while walking his dog on the mountain in 2003, and has been in regular communication with them since that time. One of the coins, he revealed, allows him to hear, see and communicate with the leprechauns.

'I can communicate with them whenever I wish. I have the gift,' he said. 'Leprechauns are spirits who can take the form of whatever we wish them to be. In my case I see them as small men, about twelve to fourteen inches in height, and they wear a suit in the traditional green of Ireland. It has gold buckles and a belt fastener.'

Every year Kevin holds a leprechaun hunt, and he has become the first person to secure planning permission for an enchanted leprechaun cavern. He discovered the underground cave, he revealed, by acting on information given to him by one of the 236 remaining leprechauns.

Kevin said in an interview: 'In a conversation, Carraig, the elder leprechaun, told me where to find the cavern. He said I had to ensure its safety.' He has fought to have the area where the leprechauns live protected by the EU under the European Habitats Directive.

Did I believe Kevin's remarkable tale? Well, as the man himself said: 'If you've lost your belief in leprechauns I believe you have lost the child in you.'

We didn't meet any leprechauns on our travels with Kevin, but we certainly had a laugh on the hunt.

***

Willowbank B&B in Enniskillen, County Fermanagh, is run by a lovely couple called Joan and Tom Foster, and they really couldn't do enough for us when we stayed with them on the journey. Willowbank is in a gorgeous setting with unspoilt views of the local lake. During our visit, Majella and I went kayaking around Enniskillen.

Then it was on to Abbeydean House, a Victorian mansion overlooking Belfast Lough in Newtownabbey, County Antrim. The owners, Tim and Ethy Clifford, are big music fans and have their entire house covered in music paraphernalia. Their display includes a life-size statue of Elvis, two jukeboxes, a gramophone, various instruments and a massive assortment of records, CDs and DVDs. They even have all my albums, most of them on vinyl!

At Abbeydean B&B we finished our first series of the show with a house party involving Tim's friends from the local rock 'n' roll club.

***

Bog racing, zorbing, ski-bobbing, ziplining, horse riding and being sere-naded in a hot tub by a male choir were just some of the experiences in our second *B&B Road Trip* series, which this time was screened by RTÉ.

In the first show we met a great character called Nancy, who owns a B&B on the doorstep of Tralee called Lee Farmhouse. She has been run-ning it for over forty years and she was full of excitement when we arrived.

Nancy is one of Ireland's original B&B owners and she is typical of the warm and inviting people who run them. Her house was shining and she had gorgeous apple tarts baked for us. She said her dream came true when I later swept her off her feet at a local dance in the Causeway outside Tralee. She goes dancing there every Sunday night.

Nancy's grandson, David, had a more challenging surprise in store for us … zorbing! You have to discard all sense of dignity to do that, as you're in a plastic bubble going around on water and trying to make headway, which I didn't do very well.

***

When we hit the road again our next stop was Gallán Mór, a boutique B&B on the Sheep's Head peninsula near Ahakista in West Cork, which was quite a buzz as it's run by two beekeepers, Noel and Lorna Burke. Their near neighbour is TV chat show star Graham Norton.

Noel and Lorna have a lovely house, set amid breathtaking scenery and sitting on a hill on the Wild Atlantic Way and with panoramic views overlooking Dunmanus Bay, Mizen Head and way out west to the Atlantic ocean. The B&B's facilities include a wood-fired hot tub, and as Majella and I enjoyed a relaxing soak in the jacuzzi al fresco we heard singing in the distance. We swivelled our heads to find the local Muintir Bhaire Men's Choir, of which Noel is a member, serenading us! We genuinely didn't know that that was going to happen, so it was a real surprise to us.

Colourful host Mona Best was eager to ensure that our Victorian-inspired stay at her quirky Bridge House B&B in Skibbereen, County Cork, was one we will never forget. Mona, who greeted us at the door wearing a white Victorian dress down to her ankles and a pink top hat, is such an unusual character. There isn't an inch of her house that doesn't have some kind of object, including mannequins, on display. She has filled her home of forty years with Victorian memorabilia, hats, clocks, plants, curtains and ornaments of every description. There was a female mannequin in our room and I put a hat over her face at night because I felt she was looking at us. Mona also left us some reading material by the bed – the Bible and *Fifty Shades of Grey*!

It was all good fun, and we also had a great night at a mad-hatters party in the local pub, The Corner Bar, which hat-loving Mona had organised. Someone said that Mona will throw a party at the drop of a hat! She dressed me up for the party as a Mexican bandit with hat, poncho and a fake moustache and beard. In The Corner Bar, Mona's lovely neighbour Valerie O'Brien got up and sang 'Red is the Rose' with me. We left the area taking great memories with us.

***

From Skibbereen it was on to Glasha Farmhouse, Ballymacarbry, County Waterford, run by mother-of-six Olive O'Gorman. Olive, a widow, is a big fan of mine and she said she was thrilled when I sang with her Nire Valley Voices choir in the local church. She was close to tears when I performed the hymn 'How Great Thou Art'. I also discovered a new talent on the O'Gorman farm, as I was given the task of milking a cow. You're never too old to learn a new skill!

In the sunny South-East we were introduced to a B&B called Anam Cara, which translates to 'Soulmate' and is located in Carriagabruce, Enniscorthy, County Wexford. It is run by a couple called Moira Fowler and Michael Cullinan, who had a very romantic story to tell.

Moira and Michael first met in the 1980s while working together at Dublin Airport and the couple fell in love. However, they drifted apart and Moira later moved to the US, where she married and made a new life for herself.

Her husband died in 2009, around the time that Michael had begun thinking about his long-lost love and had started searching for her. In good old-fashioned detective work, Michael phoned every woman with her name in the phone book until he finally hit the jackpot.

The couple had not spoken to each other in twenty-nine years, but they found that the spark was still there when they reconnected. 'I thought he was kind of cute still,' Moira said. 'You can't keep two things apart which are meant to be together, like magnets.'

Majella thought it was one of the most romantic stories she had ever heard. The couple, who opened their B&B in March 2016, took us on a falconry afternoon where I managed to overcome my fear of feathered creatures.

***

Back on the road we headed for the 'Big Smoke', where our next port of call was Aghadoe House in Glasnevin, Dublin 9. It's run by Margaret and Eugene O'Carroll, who had known each other for thirty years but had been married for just three. The couple, who also own a B&B in the Austrian ski resort of Zell am See, greeted us dressed in lederhosen and traditional Austrian costume. During our stay, they took us ski-bobbing (on bikes with skis instead of wheels) at the Ski Club of Ireland dry slope in the Dublin Mountains.

Off we went then to the west coast and an overnight stay at a unique B&B called Connemara Country Lodge, in Connemara, County Galway, where host Mary Corbett and her daughters, Stephanie and Olivia, serenade their guests at breakfast. The B&B is known as 'the home of the singing breakfast'.

Mary also introduced us to her parents, John and Bridget. It turned out that John's favourite song is 'My Donegal Shore', so I decided to sing it impromptu for him ... and John got quite emotional.

It wasn't all laid-back singing and leisurely breakfasts, as Mary then took Majella and me on a bog race! Dressed in wetsuits, we had to slide down tubes into a bog hole and then race through a muddy obstacle course. It was definitely the most challenging event we faced during the two B&B series.

Maurice and Marion Martyn's Sea Mist B&B in Galway was the perfect base from which to explore the city. The B&B opened in July 2015 with designer rooms and Marion said that running it is her dream job, but she has never worked as hard in her life. 'It's hectic, it keeps you fit but it's great craic. It's like working in the United Nations,' Marion said, referring to all the nationalities that come through her door. To cap it all we went sailing around Galway Bay in the traditional way on a Galway hooker, a boat that Majella's late father, Tom, used to enjoy sailing in. So those memories made Majella quite emotional on the trip.

Next stop was Michaeleen's Manor, in Cong, County Mayo, famously the setting for John Ford's film *The Quiet Man*, where we were guests of Gerry and Margaret Collins. Gerry and Margaret have cleverly themed their B&B around the iconic film. All six rooms are named after characters in the film. The walls are lined with photos of the stars and there are quotes from the movie above the beds.

Gerry is a super-fan of *The Quiet Man* and manages the adjacent Quiet Man Museum and Tours. He knows every line from the classic production and his family call him the 'King of the Quiet Man Crazies'.

Needless to say, it was hardly a major surprise when Majella and I found ourselves caught up in a *Quiet Man*-themed day. I was dressed up in John Wayne's familiar tweed cap and woollen waistcoat, while Majella found her inner Maureen O'Hara with a hat and shawl before we were taken on a tour in a jaunting car. Along the way we re-enacted the most famous scenes from the 1952 movie – including a kiss!

We then moved on to Clenahoo House B&B in Carrick-on-Shannon, County Leitrim, where B&B owners Noel and Deirdre Mulhern took us on a Shannon cruise on a 'Moon River' boat. While the boat meandered along we had a thoroughly enjoyable sing-song. Noel is a native of the area, while Deirdre is originally from Dublin, and they were just fantastic hosts.

As our B&B journey reached the final stages we found ourselves in Rostrevor, County Down, and a memorable stay at the superb Sands B&B, run by Anne, of the famous Sands Family of singers and musicians, and her husband John. All the Sands family gathered in the local pub for our visit and we had a hugely enjoyable sing-song with them.

Our great adventure around Ireland ended with a splash, literally, when Majella and I decided to have a water fight at Glenevin Waterfall in Donegal. I started the shenanigans, of course! Legend has it that the pool is good for fertility and has magical healing powers.

We both ended up soaking wet before we got to our destination, The Glen House B&B in Clonmany, owned by Sonia McGonigle, who declared herself to be 'a proud Donegal woman'. Try as I might, there had been no hiding my excitement when we were told that our last stop on the road trip was in Donegal and the Inishowen area. As Sonia said, there is no county like it.

Glen House is an award-winning 250-year-old guesthouse.

Sonia told me that her mother is one of my biggest fans, and all of the staff at the nine-bedroom country house were such good sports. They included Sheila Doherty, Dorothy McGonigle, Aoife McGonigle and Maggie Diver. I also met Doris Russo, an American lady who is the former owner of the guesthouse. She ran the B&B for many years and developed the walk to the near-by Glenevin Waterfall.

That afternoon we went horse riding on the local Tullagh Bay Beach. For me, it was the perfect end to a fabulous adventure.

***

We both really loved meeting all the B&B owners and it was plain to see that they were all 100 per cent committed to serving the public in their homes. Their passion shone through, and that's not something you can fake. You need to have a love of people and a joy in your work to run a business like that for a long period of your life.

We got a tremendous welcome wherever we stayed around Ireland, and I do believe that it's the same reception everyone experiences. I don't think they did anything different for us. The hospitality we enjoyed is what makes the B&B scene in Ireland so successful and so popular with the tourists and holidaymakers from at home and abroad.

I think that staying with local families is a wonderful way to see any country.

What Majella and I hoped to achieve in each half-hour show was to portray what it's like to stay in the homes of Irish people. We had a lot of fun and I have to admit that I also saw sides to Ireland that I wasn't aware of. Although I'd travelled the length and breadth of the island umpteen times as a performer, I didn't really see it with open eyes. In fact, most of the time my eyes would be shut, catching up on sleep. This time I soaked up everything that our magnificent country has to offer, from the incredible scenery to the tales and legends of local areas and the many and varied leisure activities that are waiting to be enjoyed.

Until we did the B&B show, Majella had never stayed in one, so it was a new experience for her. She loved it, of course, because what's not to like about them?

'My God, the value you get is amazing, and the attention you receive is second to none,' Majella said in an interview. 'If you are a foreigner coming here on holiday and you want to experience Ireland you should definitely stay in a B&B. In a hotel you are anonymous and you float in and out without anyone paying attention to you. In the B&Bs you feel like you are part of their family.'

Since we did the series, there have been reports of a huge increase in business for the B&Bs. I'm delighted to hear it. They really are a wonderful asset to Irish tourism.

CHAPTER 21

OFF TO SEA

I have spent my adult life touring the world as a singer and entertainer. For the most part, it has been a hectic whirl: negotiating busy airports, catching connecting flights, going on road trips, checking in and out of hotels, doing afternoon sound checks at concert venues and sold-out shows at night.

After Majella was diagnosed with breast cancer and underwent chemotherapy and a double mastectomy in 2014, I decided that when she recovered I would take a long break from my high-flying career so that we could enjoy some quality time together at a leisurely pace.

In January 2016 we embarked on the holiday of a lifetime … a four-month luxury cruise around the world. We didn't do the entire world, but we got around half of it and it was definitely a once-in-a-lifetime experience that we will never forget. They say that travel broadens the mind, and we certainly learned a lot and visited places I never, ever dreamt as a child that I would get to see in person. Even going on a world cruise was something that, way back in my youth, I associated with Hollywood stars.

I had been on cruise ships as a singer and loved the lifestyle, as did Majella. Before I went on a cruise for the first time I wasn't sure if I would enjoy it, but you are treated like royalty on board. I have since been on different cruises and loved every one of them. I have also worked with a lady called Gertrude Byrne, who runs an 'All Star Irish Cruise' in the Caribbean every year. That is a week-long cruise with other entertainers and it is always so much fun.

However, my world cruise with Majella was total escapism. With no work for four months, we quickly settled into an idyllic life of luxury, leisure and the exploration of other cultures in exotic locations around the globe.

When I got up in the morning I enjoyed the fact that I had nothing to do only organise my day whatever way I wanted. Every morning began with breakfast and afterwards I regularly attended Mass on board ship. This was then followed by a bridge lesson when the ship was at sea. I had always wanted to learn how to play bridge, and I finally got the opportunity on the cruise. Any day that we were travelling and not docked in a port there was a bridge class. There was a lesson in the morning and then at two in the afternoon you played a game.

After three weeks of doing the lessons I ventured into my first ever bridge game. The pressure of it was so great that I thought my head was going to burst. I had to go back to the cabin when it was all over and take a headache pill. However, I persevered with the game, eventually got the hang of it and I loved it from then on.

Majella, meanwhile, went to art classes, enjoyed some pampering in the spa or relaxed with some reading. We also had the option of lying in the sun and topping up our tans at one of the two outdoor pools on the ship.

However, with top-class cuisine on offer for breakfast, lunch and dinner, we made sure to put in some time in the gym every day. There were half-hour classes in the morning and evening with all kinds of workouts and body toning. We did the treadmill for half an hour most days. That allowed us to eat whatever we wanted, and we ate plenty. The gym is a distant memory now, and I'm afraid everything has fallen to where it used to be.

There was also a daily group trivia quiz. That was highly competitive. There were ten of us on each team. I was baffled by the questions most of the time, as you wouldn't hear the like of them on *Mastermind*, but on the very last day I knew the answer to a question that helped my team win the overall quiz.

What was the question? It was to name the characters played by Jason Donovan and Kylie Minogue in the TV soap *Neighbours*. I wasn't an avid watcher of Neighbours, but I recalled correctly that their characters were Scott and Charlene. As nobody else had the answer right, we got double points. After all the days of contributing very little I came up with the right answer at the right time, so I was well pleased with myself.

Our holiday was with a cruise line called Seabourn and we travelled on two of their ships, the *Seabourn Odyssey* and *Seabourn Sojourn*. We did the trip in two legs, with our first journey taking forty days from Los Angeles to Sydney, across the Pacific Ocean, down through the French Polynesian islands.

French Polynesia comprises more than 100 islands in the South Pacific. We got off the boat at one of the islands and, while taking a stroll with

Majella, I spotted a glitter ball in a garden so I trotted over and threw my arms around it. I didn't win the glitter ball on *Strictly Come Dancing*, unfortunately, but at least I got my hands on one in French Polynesia.

We also dropped into Papeete, the capital of French Polynesia and the hub of its tourism. The commune of Papeete is located on the island of Tahiti, the largest of the islands that make up French Polynesia.

As the cruise continued, along the way we crossed the date line, so we lost a day. Then we went to New Zealand and sailed across one of their stunning natural attractions, Milford Sound, enjoying its dramatic landscapes. We docked in Tasmania where we visited Burnie.

I have performed on tour in Hobart, Tasmania, but this was my first time in Burnie, a port on the north-west coast. It's named after William Burnie, a director of Van Diemen's Land Company in the early 1840s. We got off the ship and strolled through the centre of the town, which reminded me of Dungloe and other small towns in Ireland. They tick along without causing a great stir, but at the same time they are functioning for people who live within reach of them. We visited the local museum and enjoyed checking out the history of how Burnie had evolved through the decades.

Back on board ship we set sail for Sydney, the final destination of that leg. Sydney Harbour is one of the most incredible places in the world. It's surrounded by hundreds of kilometres of shoreline, national parks and historic sites. Even though I have been to Sydney many times on tour, arriving into the harbour on a cruise ship gave me a totally different perspective. There are many beautiful homes to be seen around the bay.

Sydney Harbour, of course, is home to the magnificent Sydney Opera House, where I have been fortunate to perform in concert. This iconic structure sits out in the harbour, making such a statement. As we were sailing by I said to Majella: 'That's one of the wonders of the world – the dressing room where I changed for my show!'

From Sydney we flew to Singapore, where we boarded another Sea-bourn ship to begin our next adventure. This one took us all around South East Asia, South Korea and Myanmar. In Myanmar, formerly Burma, I was struck by the enormous gulf between the very rich and the very poor. You see incredible poverty side by side with incredible wealth. There are more than 100 ethnic groups in this nation which borders India, Bangladesh, China, Laos and Thailand. We had a guide taking us around and we visited one of the oldest temples. Then we stopped off at The Grand Hotel where people were dining and it was almost colonial. India was like that too.

On we went then by ship to Taiwan, Vietnam, Cambodia and Thailand, where we stopped off on the gorgeous Phuket Island. However, as Majella and I strolled around this paradise in Thailand I couldn't help but think back to the 2004 Indian Ocean earthquake and tsunami which killed at least 250 people in Phuket, and more than 5400 overall in Thailand.

As I was walking on the beach I remembered reading how the sea goes out when a tsunami happens, and then it comes back in with devastating force. Some of the people that day walked out where the sea had been, not realising what was happening and that it was about to return. On the day we visited we stood and remembered the tragedy that had happened.

Our journey continued to Malaysia and the Philippines. No matter where you go in the world you are sure to encounter a fellow Irish man or woman, and on the cruise we met a Dubliner called Kevin who lives in Manila in the Philippines. Kevin and his partner gave Majella and myself a personal tour of Manila for two days during our stopover on the cruise. It was fantastic to have someone with local knowledge and local contacts.

One of the local attractions we visited was Malacanang Palace, the first residence of the President of the Philippines. It's open to the public, but we actually got to enter rooms where tourists don't normally gain access thanks to our local guides.

Back on the ship, we headed on to China and Japan. On our visit to Japan, Majella and I went native! As we got off the cruise ship there was the opportunity to get dressed up in the local costume for a souvenir picture. Naturally we took up the offer, so I was snapped with my very own Geisha girl … Majella!

On that stop, we visited Ha Long Bay in northern Vietnam, 170 km east of Hanoi, which is a popular tourist area. The bay is often included in lists of natural wonders of the world. It is a UNESCO World Heritage Site that has some 1600 islands and islets, forming a spectacular seascape of limestone pillars. Most of the islands are uninhabited and unaffected by a human presence.

We saw the villages where people lived and fished and spent their whole lives in this sheltered part of the sea. Their traditions are now dying out, but it was amazing to see how they once existed.

We also took a trip to see the Hiroshima Peace Memorial Park, which is dedicated to the legacy of Hiroshima, the first city in the world to suffer a nuclear attack on 6 August 1945. It also remembers the bomb's direct and indirect victims, of whom there may have been as many as 140,000.

The park is built on an open field that was created by the explosion. There is a Peace Bell near the Children's Peace Monument, which is a large Japanese bell hanging inside a small open-sided structure. Visitors are encouraged to ring the bell for world peace.

Finally our cruise took us up to Brunei and Oman before our last stop in

Dubai and the end of our grand global adventure on sea and land.

The sights we saw, the people we met and the different cultures we encountered were amazing experiences we will never forget. We realise how fortunate we are to have been in a position both financially and time-wise to do it. We will probably never take a trip on that scale again, but we will definitely go on more cruises. A cruise is total escapism and a lovely way to spend a holiday.

CHAPTER 22

ON THE ROAD
AGAIN

A hurricane greeted my return to the live concert scene in December 2015.

That weekend, as tickets were going on sale for my series of shows the following August in Killarney, County Kerry, Ireland was being battered and bruised by ferocious winds. And the rain that came tumbling out of the skies was of biblical proportions.

Storm Desmond had come roaring in like a prehistoric creature roused from its sleep, at a time when I was hoping that people would be talking about Storm Daniel.

But there you go: people make plans and God smiles, as they say.

On the Friday night, 4 December, I did a TV performance on *The Late Late Show* in Dublin. Then I hopped in a car with my manager, Kieran Cavanagh, and off we went into the night and the eye of a storm for a journey of several turbulent hours to Killarney.

Although tickets were going to be available online the following day, they were also set to be sold at the box office in Killarney's INEC venue. As it was a special event for me, I had arranged to be there in person to meet fans who turned up for their tickets.

I had been very excited about this special event in the build-up to it, but then Storm Desmond arrived to spoil the party. As the rain pounded off the windscreen and the car rocked in the wind along the journey, I thought to myself: well, nobody is going to turn up in Killarney in the morning, because who would be foolish enough to go out in weather like this?

When I shared my thoughts with Kieran, he was more optimistic.

It was 2.30am when we eventually arrived safely at our hotel after one of the worst journeys that I can remember. It really had been a frightful night to be out. However, I had made a promise to be at the INEC on that morning, and even if only two people turned up they would have expected me to be there.

Imagine my surprise, then, the following morning when a chirpy Kieran rang my room to say that hundreds of people were at the venue and looking forward to meeting me. I was absolutely overwhelmed by the turnout in such atrocious weather, and so delighted to meet those people.

The first two tickets were purchased by a lovely couple who revealed to the *Sunday World* newspaper that they had met three years earlier on a Gertrude Byrne Caribbean Cruise where I was one of the entertainers.

Kieran Burke, aged 77, from Douglas, County Cork, and Jean Mullane, aged 73, from Chicago told the paper that they were both fans of my music. Both had lost their partners in life, and neither was looking for love when they went on the Caribbean cruise and came to my shows.

Jean told the journalist Eddie Rowley that she had been a fan of my music since she first saw me perform in her native city of Chicago nearly thirty years previously.

'I've been to see Daniel about twenty times in concert, mostly in America, but many times in Ireland too,' Jean said. 'I've been on two cruises where Daniel was the performer and I've been to see his shows in Branson, Missouri.

'My Irish-born husband died thirteen years ago after forty years of marriage, so I was on my own on a cruise around the Caribbean nearly three years ago when I met this very nice Cork man.

'I went on the cruise because Daniel was the main entertainer on the ship. So I guess Danny waved his magic wand when I met Kieran.'

Kieran, a widower for 32 years, said he wasn't looking for love when he went on the cruise. 'I was looking for a pint at the time, but they don't have pints on those cruises. Instead, I found this very nice lady,' he laughed, as he recalled his first encounter with Jean in the same newspaper interview.

'Jean is lovely and I've met all her family in Chicago. Her adult children run a famous Irish dancing academy there. We both travel over and back to see each other as often as we can, even though we're not chickens now, the two of us.'

Kieran said he has been a fan of my music since 1998. 'Daniel performs for over three hours at his concerts, he's great craic, and I love the duets he does with Mary Duff. Afterwards, he meets his customers, so you always go home feeling you've had a great night. It's a great morning here as well and has been well worth the effort to make the trip. There is always a good atmosphere around functions organised by Daniel,' he added.

Another fan, Mark Bryan (39), accompanied by his sister, Annette (42) and their twelve-year-old niece Chloe Cronin, had set off from Bandon, County Cork, at 2.30am to meet me at the INEC and to get their tickets for the concert the following year.

'I know people will think we're mad, but it's brilliant craic here this morning with Daniel and well worth the effort to get here,' Mark told the newspaper. 'My niece has been following Daniel since she was three. My sister was always a fan of Daniel and she kept insisting that I should go to his show. To keep her quiet I eventually went to a Daniel concert and I was then hooked. Now I go to all of his concerts in Ireland and I travel to see him in the UK as well. I've even been to see him in the Royal Albert Hall in London. He's probably sick looking at us at this stage.'

With the tickets then selling out, I had those shows to look forward to the following August. There would be a world cruise to enjoy in the meantime, but time flies and before I knew it, August 2016 was upon me.

***

I had a tear in my eye going back to work with my band after being off the road for a year and a half.

This was nothing to do with my holidays being over after all that time away from the stage. It was the reminder as I sang 'My Donegal Shore' in rehearsals of just how privileged and lucky I was to still have the opportunity to do a job that I love. It had all started with 'My Donegal Shore' in 1983. Now here I was thirty-three years later, rehearsing that song with my new band as the next stage of the journey was about to kick off.

Of course, I never think of singing and performing as work or a job. But there is a big responsibility that comes with it as you always want to give audiences your best show, so we all knuckled down to rehearsals in the weeks leading up to the first concert.

When we gathered together in a rehearsal studio outside Dublin, somebody remarked that we looked like Bruce Springsteen's E Street Band.

My new band was a mixture of musicians who had been with me in the past, as well as six people who were joining me for the first time.

Although I was familiar with the newcomers, it took a while to really get to know each other. The new musicians in the group had a lot of songs to learn, so it was a big challenge for them. I've always had a great band around me and I knew in the early stages of the rehearsals that the new guys were going to freshen up the show and bring a different dynamic to it. Their ability and their dedication were fantastic.

The six new members were James Blennerhassett (bass), Jim McVeigh (accordion/piano), Mick McCarney (lead/rhythm guitar), Stevie Hamilton (guitar/banjo), Des Lacey (drums/percussion) and Kane O'Rourke, a multi-instrumentalist who plays everything bar the sittingroom settee.

Mary Duff, of couse, was back as my touring partner, and the line-up was completed by Trionagh Allen on backing vocals and Stephen Milne on piano and strings.

The rehearsals with Mary and all the gang were good fun. I felt a little bit rusty vocally at the start because the voice is like a muscle and you need to keep working it, so it takes a while to warm up after a long rest.

But every day as we worked on the new show it got better and better, and I knew that by the time we opened in Killarney I'd be singing like a bird again.

***

The moment I stepped out on stage to the applause of the audience on opening night at Killarney's INEC that August, I felt elated and a sense of being 'home'. I've said many times that there is no place I feel more at home than on a stage. I just love it. Even though I had taken the longest period off since the start of my career, my first night on stage in Killarney was like meeting an old friend after many months or years. You just pick up the conversation where you last left off. It's like no time had elapsed in between.

As ever, the fans were just fantastic and their enthusiasm and engagement every night made the shows so enjoyable for me. People had come from many places around the world for my comeback in Killarney that summer. And many of them attended the concerts every night. I couldn't have asked for a better welcome back.

Once I took off again there was no stopping me, as our tour schedule for 2016 and 2017 took us around the world. One of my favourite places to play is Branson, Missouri, where I do a residency in a local theatre every year. Majella and I even bought a little cabin there as our home from home when I'm in town to do my shows. It's nice to have somewhere familiar to stay and a place to leave our clothes and other accessories when we are stationed there on tour.

I started going to America on tour in 1990, and in the beginning it was a slow burner. America is a very daunting place to build a career. It's so vast that getting your name known is like climbing Mount Everest. I used to think that I would have a better chance of climbing Mount Everest, but my then manager Sean Reilly never lost faith and believed that if we persevered we would finally find our audience in that part of the world.

Then in 2002 I had my first show aired on public television (PBS) across America, and that gained an audience straight away. With the support of PBS, ten shows sold out in the Mickey Gilley Theatre in Branson before we got there, and it has been growing ever since. I remember when I first visited Branson and went to the Andy Williams Theatre with Sean Reilly, I said, 'Maybe some day I'll do shows here.' Then I got the opportunity to play there. It's sad that Andy Williams is no longer with us. I do feel quite privileged, though, that I got to meet Andy during my years performing in Branson and I found him to be an absolute gentleman.

Very few Irish artists have made the breakthrough in America, and journalists often ask me what is the secret of my success. Like all things, certainly you have to have some talent that God has given you, but there need to be lucky breaks. Getting our shows on PBS television in America was our big break. I was forty-one in 2002 when it took off for me in America, so I was no teenager. There were times in the early days when I would have given up on the American dream. Sean Reilly persuaded me to keep on trying and he kept on chipping away until we got our break with PBS. Sean had the faith that it would happen for me in America and Canada; he was the one driving it and in the end we saw the dream come to life.

***

Sri Lanka, an island in the Indian Ocean, is another nation that has taken me to its heart, and I was back there performing in March 2017.

I had no idea that I had an audience in Sri Lanka until a few years ago when Cliff Richard was performing in that beautiful part of the world. In 2006, as I have mentioned, I was one of the artists who duetted with Cliff on his album *Two's Company – The Duets*. We recorded The Carpenters' song 'Yesterday Once More'. Later, when Cliff was on tour in Sri Lanka, he introduced the song one night on stage by saying:

'This is a song I recorded with an Irish singer called Daniel O'Donnell.' There was a burst of applause from the audience and it took Cliff by surprise.

'Do you know Daniel O'Donnell?' Cliff asked. There was a big cheer again, confirming that, yes indeed, they did know Daniel O'Donnell.

Well, that was news to me when Cliff phoned me with the story of what had transpired during his show.

'Do you know that they all know you here in Sri Lanka?' he asked.

Up to that moment I hadn't heard a whisper about my music being popular in Sri Lanka. And if you asked me then, I couldn't have pointed out the location of Sri Lanka on a map.

'The local promoter here wants you to do some shows, so you need to do something about it and get out here,' Cliff added.

Sean Reilly checked it out and, sure enough, the promoter offered us some shows. We discovered that my records had become big in Sri Lanka thanks to my songs being played on a radio station there called Gold FM.

I would then meet Sri Lankan people in the UK and Australia and they also told me that I was very popular in their homeland. One lady informed me that once every hour one of my records is played on the radio there.

Country music in general, I later learned, is very popular in Sri Lanka.

The people there love the late American country legend Jim Reeves and, of course, I did a Jim Reeves tribute album in the past.

When I first performed in Sri Lanka I couldn't believe the reception I received. It really was overwhelming. You'd think I was Michael Jackson! The Sri Lankans are a lovely, warm, gentle race of people who embraced me like one of their own.

On our 2017 tour, I noticed that songs like the Irish ballads 'Galway Bay' and 'The Isle of Inisfree' were particularly popular with the Sri Lankan fans. 'You By My Side' was another favourite, and they loved the duets I did with my touring partner Mary Duff. They are really taken with Mary in that part of the world too.

While performing in Sri Lanka in this year of 2017 I was reminded of many things.

It made me reflect on the journey of my life, from the little fishing village of Kincasslagh to recognition and success in the unlikeliest of places around the world.

Music is such a common language and it makes the same connection with people, whether they are in Ireland or Sri Lanka or any of the other countries that I perform in around the globe.

I was also reminded of the fact that people's lives are basically the same the world over. We all go through similar struggles: we share the circle of life from births to deaths, love and loss, joy and heartache, success and failure.

It's all in the music and in the songs. What a grey life it would be without music. And what a difference music has made to my life.

I hope it enriches your life too.

DISCOGRAPHY

Back Home Again (2017)

Disc 1: Never Ending Song of Love * Back Home Again * The Galway Shawl * Why Don't You Love Me (Like You Used to Do) * Love Letters in the Sand * Pretty Little Girl from Omagh * Silver Threads and Golden Needles (*Mary Duff*) * Mr Noble (*Mary Duff*) * It Doesn't Matter Anymore (*duet with Mary Duff*) * Just Someone I Used to Know (*duet with Mary Duff*) * Things * The Mountains of Mourne * Irish Air (tin whistle)/Fiddler's Green (*duet with Mary Duff*) /Fiddle Tune/The River Shannon (*Mary Duff*)

Disc 2: I Just Want to Dance With You * Memory Number One * The Boys from Killybegs * Song for the Mira * On the Eighth Day * Hold Onto Your Hat (*Derek Ryan*) * You're Only Young Once (*Derek Ryan*) * God's Plan (*duet with Derek Ryan*) * Cotton Fields Back Home (*with Mary Duff and Derek Ryan*) * I Won't Be Home No More * There's a Blue Moon Over My World * Without You * Me and Bobby McGee * Help Me Make It Through the Night (*duet with Mary Duff*) * Home to Donegal * Stand Beside Me * Our House Is a Home * Tipperary Girl * How Great Thou Art * Until the Next Time

I Have a Dream (2016)

Everything Is Beautiful * Never Ending Song of Love * Beautiful Sunday * Sweet Caroline * I Can See Clearly Now * Help Me Make It Through the Night * For the Good Times * Lucille * Raindrops Keep Falling on My Head * Top of the World (*duet with Mary Duff*) * Honey * The Most Beautiful Girl * Can't Help Falling in Love * Spanish Eyes * You Needed Me * I Have a Dream * You're My Best Friend (*duet with Mary Duff*) * Knock Three Times * Living Next Door to Alice * Is This the Way to Amarillo

The Ultimate Irish Album (2016)

Disc 1: Tipperary Girl * Pretty Little Girl from Omagh * The Mountains of Mourne * The Galway Shawl * My Donegal Shore * Sing Me an Old Irish Song * Moon Over Ireland * The Old Dungarvan Oak * Mary from Dungloe * Forty Shades of Green * Cottage by the Lee * The Isle of Innisfree * Far, Far from Home * Danny Boy * The Boys from Killybegs * Home to Donegal * An Irish Lullaby * My Lovely Rose of Clare * Blue Hills of Breffni * Belfast

Disc 2: My Wild Irish Rose * Heaven Around Galway Bay * Home Is Where the Heart Is * Limerick You're a Lady * Irish Eyes * Four Country Roads * Sonny * An Exile's Dream * Destination Donegal * Red Is the Rose * Green Willow * Among the Wicklow Hills * Eileen * Lough Melvin's Rocky Shore * Galway Bay * My Father's House * Green Glens of Antrim * Pat Murphy's Meadow * My Bonnie Maureen * I'll Take You Home Again Kathleen

Disc 3: The Fields of Athenry * Our House Is a Home * My Lovely Donegal * Dublin in the Rare Auld Times * Come Back Paddy Reilly to Ballyjamesduff * Any Tipperary Town * When You Were Sweet Sixteen * The Green Hills of Sligo * Roads of Kildare * Maggie * Sweet Forget Me Not * The Rose of Mooncoin * Your Friendly Irish Way * Cutting the Corn in Creeslough * Dear Old Galway Town * Home Town on the Foyle * The Banks of My Own Lovely Lee * My Lovely Island Home * Moonlight in Mayo * The Town I Loved So Well

The Hank Williams Songbook (2015)

Jambalaya * Half as Much * Hey, Good Lookin' * You Win Again * Why Don't You Love Me (Like You Used to Do) * Your Cheatin' Heart * Let's Turn Back the Years * I Can't Help It (If I'm Still in Love With You) * Kaw-Liga * Take These Chains from My Heart * Wedding Bells * I Won't Be Home No More * My Son Calls Another Man Daddy * Cold, Cold Heart * A Mansion on the Hill * I Saw the Light

Best of Music & Memories (2015)

Disc 1: Welcome to My World * From a Jack to a King * Our House Is a Home (*studio version 2014*) * I Just Want to Dance with You * Moon River * Geisha Girl * Sing Me an Old Irish Song * Help Me Make It Through the Night * I'll Fly Away * Whispering Hope (*duet with Mary Duff*) * Halfway to Paradise * Wherever You Are * Our Anniversary (*studio version 2014*) * My Shoes Keep Walking Back to You * Heaven With You * You're My Best Friend (*duet with Mary Duff*) * My Happiness (*duet with Mary Duff*) **Disc 2**: Only This Moment Is Mine * Rosa Rio * It's a Long Way to Tipperary/Pack Up Your Troubles/If You're Irish, Come into the Parlour * Tennessee Waltz * Que Sera Sera * Walk Tall * I Saw the Light * Wind beneath My Wings * Try a Little Kindness * There Goes My Everything * King of the Road * Could I Have This Dance * Stand Beside Me (*studio version 2014*) * Home to Donegal * Daydream Believer * I Saw the Light

Stand Beside Me (2014)
Disc 1: Stand Beside Me * Que Sera Sera * A Picture of You * Take Good Care of Her * Erin Tennessee * Flying With Angels * Hey Mr Moon * Eileen McManus (*duet with Mary Duff*) * Everybody's Somebody's Fool (*Mary Duff*) * Just Out of Reach (*Mary Duff*) * I Heard the Bluebirds Sing (*duet with Mary Duff*) * Home I'll Be * Walk Tall * Our Anniversary * Perfect Days * Moon Over Ireland * Rose Garden (*Mary Duff*) * Beautiful Sunday * Sweet Caroline * Da Doo Ron Ron **Disc 2**: Do What You Do Do Well * My Father's House (*with Mary Duff and Kevin Sheerin*) * Dear God (*Mary Duff*) * Lara's Theme * Roll Out the Barrel * Silver Wings (*Nigel Connell, Trionagh Allen and Leon McCrum*) * It's Hard to Be Humble (*duet with John Staunton*) * Teetotaller's Reel * Boys of Blue Hill * Together Again (*duet with Mary Duff*) * Blaze of Glory * That's Amore * God's Plan * Wooden Heart * The Fields of Athenry * Daddy's Hands (*Mary Duff*) * South of the Border * A White Sport Coat * I Just Want Dance with You * It's a Long Way to Tipperary * Pack Up Your Troubles * If You're Irish, Come into the Parlour * The Blackthorn Stick * Stand Beside Me (*reprise*) * Rivers of Babylon * How Great Thou Art

The Inspirational Collection (2014)
Disc 1: Footsteps * It Is No Secret * Morning Has Broken * I Watch the Sunrise * You Raise Me Up * Why Me Lord * You Needed Me * My Forever Friend * One Day at a Time * When Darkness Falls * Beyond the Rainbow's End * I Believe * Let It Be * Sweet Queen of Peace * Abide With Me * Softly and Tenderly * Let There Be Peace * Marriage of a Lifetime * The Rose * The Old Rugged Cross
Disc 2: I Saw the Light * Annie's Song * Nearer My God to Thee * You'll Never Walk Alone * Wind beneath My Wings * Be Not Afraid * Here I Am Lord * What a Friend

We Have in Jesus * Make Me a Channel of Your Peace * Sweet Heart of Jesus * At the End of the Day * Only a Shadow of Your Love * Battle Hymn of the Republic * Surely the Presence of the Lord * God Be with You till We Meet Again * Light a Candle * Going Home * Holy God, We Praise Thy Name * Amazing Grace * How Great Thou Art

From the Heartland (2013)
Stand Beside Me * On the Wings of a Dove * Okie from Muskogee * When You Were Sweet Sixteen * Detroit City * Pick Me Up on Your Way Down (*Mary Duff*) * Only This Moment Is Mine * Far Side Banks of Jordan * Don't Let Me Cross Over * I'm Just Lucky I Guess * Maggie * Moon River * Geisha Girl * Standing Room Only * Sonny's Dream * Distant Drums * Blanket on the Ground (*duet with Mary Duff*) * Our House Is a Home * Rivers of Babylon * How Great Thou Art

A Picture of You (2013)
Another Somebody Done Somebody Wrong Song * Hey Mr Moon * Moon River * Perfect Days * Penny Arcade * If I Didn't Have a Dime * The Most Beautiful Girl in the World * Darlin' * God's Plan * I Can't Help Falling in Love With You * Walk Tall * The Band Played an Old Time Waltz * A Picture of You * Love Letters in the Sand * Our Anniversary * Home I'll Be

The Rock 'n' Roll Years (2013)
Disc 1: I'm a Believer * Daydream Believer * Do You Wanna Dance * Sweet Caroline * Be My Guest * Singing the Blues * Young Love * You're Sixteen * Girl of My Best Friend * Love Me Tender * Blueberry Hill * Bye Bye Love * Save the Last Dance for Me * Sealed With a Kiss * Twelfth of Never * Roses Are Red * Travellin' Light * Rhythm of the Rain * Hello Mary Lou * Teenager in Love
Disc 2: That'll Be the Day * Beautiful Sunday * Let's Dance * Three Steps to Heaven * Is This the Way to Amarillo * Let's Twist Again * Calendar Girl * But I Do * Good Luck Charm * My Special Angel * Halfway to Paradise * Come on Over to My Place * Wonderful Tonight * Walk Right Back * When * Only Sixteen * Oh Boy * And Then I Kissed Her * Da Doo Ron Ron * Living Next Door to Alice

Songs from the Movies & More (2012)

Somewhere My Love * Raindrops Keep Falling on My Head * That's Amore * Black Hills of Dakota * South of the Border * Cowboy's Lament (*Streets of Laredo*) * Que Sera Sera * A White Sport Coat * Home on the Range * Don't Fence Me In * Cool Water * Red River Valley * A Little Bitty Tear * Edelweiss * Singin' in the Rain * We'll Meet Again

The Ultimate Collection (2011)

Disc 1: Welcome to My World * Love Is a Beautiful Song * I Just Want to Dance With You * My Donegal Shore * You Raise Me Up * Footsteps * I Need You * Tipperary Girl * Four Country Roads * Heaven With You * Beyond the Rainbow's End * Danny Boy * Teenager in Love * I'd Live My Life Over With You * Stand Beside Me * Still You * Red Is the Rose * Crush on You * Tennessee Waltz * Erin Tennessee (*live*)

Disc 2: Whatever Happened to Old Fashioned Love * Peace in the Valley * My Shoes Keep Walking Back to You * Wind beneath My Wings * I'm Going to Be a Country Boy Again * Take Good Care of Her * Can You Feel the Love * Moon Over Ireland * Flying With Angels * Don't Forget to Remember * Dream Lover * Song for the Mira * Can't Hold the Years Back * Only This Moment Is Mine * Marianne * Poetry in Motion * Make the World Go Away * Love Is Everything * Here at the Grand Ole Opry (*live*) * How Great Thou Art

Moon Over Ireland (2011)

Moon Over Ireland * When You Were Sweet Sixteen * The Fields of Athenry * Tipperary Girl * The Galway Shawl * My Father's House * My Wild Irish Rose * Moonlight in Mayo * Maggie * Sonny's Dream * Two Little Orphans * Cottage by the Lee * Red Is the Rose * The Boys from Killybegs * My Lovely Donegal * The Town I Loved So Well

O Holy Night (2010)

Mary's Boy Child * Angels We Have Heard on High * O Little Town of Bethlehem * Little Drummer Boy * O Come All Ye Faithful * Mary Did You Know? * Away in a Manger * Hark the Herald Angels Sing * O Holy Night * Remember Me * Silent Night * Once in Royal David's City * The First Noel * In the Bleak Midwinter * Christmas Day 1915

Peace in the Valley (2009)

Peace in the Valley * Mansion Over the Hilltop * Far Side Banks of Jordan * On the Wings of a Dove * If Jesus Comes Tomorrow, What Then? * Wait a Little Longer, Please Jesus * Precious Memories * If I Could Hear My Mother Pray Again * Just a Closer Walk With Thee * A Satisfied Mind * I Won't Have to Cross Jordan Alone * The Church in the Wildwood * Praying * Where We Never Grow Old * I'll Fly Away

Hope & Praise (2009)

Disc 1: Why Me Lord * Love, Hope & Faith * Morning Has Broken * Let There Be Peace * Footsteps * What a Wonderful World * Any Dream Will Do * Voice of an Angel (*Mary Duff*) * Abide With Me * Put Your Hand in the Hand * Hail Glorious Saintt Patrick * Children's Band * When Hope Dawns at Sunrise * I Believe

Disc 2: I'll Fly Away * Whispering Hope (*duet with Mary Duff*) * Will You Walk With Me (*Mary Duff*) * A Little Peace * Beyond the Rainbow's End * Annie's Song * The Greatest Love * Marriage of a Lifetime * You'll Never Walk Alone * Rivers of Babylon * God Be With You

The Rock 'n' Roll Show Live (2008)

Disc 1: Come on Over to My Place * Oh Boy * When You Walk in the Room * Three Steps to Heaven * Twelfth of Never * That'll Be the Day * Poetry in Motion * My Boy Lollipop (*Mary Duff*) * C'est La Vie/You Never Can Tell (*Mary Duff*) * Walk Right Back (*duet with Mary Duff*) * Calendar Girl * Elvis Medley: Blue Suede Shoes/Good Luck Charm/Love Me Tender/All Shook Up * Words * Teenager in Love * Lipstick on Your Collar (*Mary Duff*) * Johnny B. Goode (*Mary Duff*)

Disc 2: Beautiful Sunday * Wonderful Tonight * You're Sixteen * Girl of My Best Friend * Hopelessly Devoted to You (*Mary Duff*) * Beatles Medley: All My Loving/ Hey Jude/Yesterday/Ticket to Ride * (Is This the Way to) Amarillo * The Moon of Love Medley: Dream Lover/Single Girl/I'm a Believer/Bobby's Girl/When/Don't Go Breaking My Heart/Shoop Shoop Song/Da Doo Ron Ron/Then I Kissed Her/Under the Moon of Love * Jail House Rock (*Billy Burgoyne*) * Only Sixteen

Disc 3: Be My Guest * Ole Man Trouble * Knock Three Times * Where the Boys Are * The Carnival Is Over (*duet with Mary Duff*) * I Don't Know Why I Love You But I Do * Daydream Believer * Donna * At the Hop * Cliff Richard Medley: Living Doll/

Young Ones/Summer Holiday/Miss You Nights/Do You Want to Dance * Walking Back to Happiness (*Mary Duff*) * Ob-La-Di, Ob-La-Da * Living Next Door to Alice * Rockin' Robin (*Mary Duff*) * Let's Twist Again * Let's Dance * Rock Around the Clock

Country Boy (2008)
I'm Going to Be a Country Boy Again * If I Said You Had a Beautiful Body, Would You Hold It Against Me * Lucille * Back Home Again * Me and Bobby McGee * King of the Road * Little Ole Wine Drinker Me * Release Me * From Here to There to You * Detroit City * I Wanna Be Free (*duet with Loretta Lynn*) * Mother's Birthday Song * Crystal Chandeliers (*duet with Charley Pride*) * Seven Spanish Angels * Ring of Fire * He Stopped Loving Her Today * Okie from Muskogee * I'm Just Lucky I Guess * Could I Have This Dance for the Rest of My Life * Oh Lonesome Me

Through the Years (2008)
Disc 1: Celtic Memories: The Rose of Mooncoin * Galway Bay * Irish Eyes * Limerick You're a Lady * Any Tipperary Town * Mary from Dungloe * Forty Shades of Green * Pat Murphy's Meadow * Home Is Where the Heart Is * Danny Boy * I'll Take You Home Again Kathleen * Three Leaf Shamrock * Dublin in the Rare Auld Times * These Are My Mountains * An Irish Lullaby
Disc 2: Songs of Devotion: Annie's Song * Light a Candle * The Rose * Let It Be * Panis Angelicus * I Saw the Light * Love, Hope and Faith * Follow Your Dream * I Need You * I Believe * A Song for the World * What a Wonderful World * You Raise Me Up * A Little Piece of Heaven * How Great Thou Art
Disc 3: Romantic Moments: Whatever Happened to Old Fashioned Love * The Love in Your Eyes * Leaving Is Easy (When Loving Is Hard) * I Wonder Where You Are Tonight * My Dreams Just Came True * Don't Forget to Remember * Crying My Heart Out Over You * Help Me Make It through the Night * Love Me Tender * Some Day You'll Want Me to Want You * It Comes and Goes * Broken Hearts Always Mend * Old Loves Never Die * Take Good Care of Her * I Can't Help It (If I'm Still In Love With You)
Disc 4: Traditional Favourites: The Magic Is There * Save the Last Dance for Me * Four in the Morning * A Fool Such As I * Excuse Me (I Think I've Got a Heartache) * Don't Let Me Cross Over * You Know I Still Love You * Before I'm Over You * Make

the World Go Away * She Goes Walking Through My Mind * Tennessee Waltz * The Way That You Are * Yesterday's Memories * Roses Are Red * Welcome to My World

At Home in Ireland (2008)

Disc 1: Stand Beside Me * Oh Lonesome Me * Sweet Forget Me Not * Dear Old Galway Town * Destination Donegal * Burning Bridges * Foolin' Around * I Forgot to Remember to Forget You * It Is No Secret * There Goes My Everything * Do You Think You Could Love Me Again * Heartaches by the Number * The Blue Hills of Breffni

Disc 2: Happy Birthday Tribute * My Lovely Island Home * If Anything Happened to You (*Mary Duff*) * Try a Little Kindness * Belfast City * I've Got a Tiger By the Tail * Second Fiddle * I Missed Me * Little Arrows * My Lovely Rose of Clare * Working Man (*Mary Duff*) * Save Your Love (*duet with Mary Duff*) * Medley: You Are My Sunshine/It Takes a Worried Man/Down By the Riverside/You Are My Sunshine

Together Again (with Mary Duff) (2007)

Together Again * Top of the World * The Carnival Is Over * My Happiness * Are You Teasing Me * Timeless and True Love * You're My Best Friend * Hey Good Lookin' * Harbour Lights * Do You Think You Could Love Me Again * Til' a Tear Becomes a Rose * I Don't Care * Yes, Mr Peters * Daddy Was an Old Time Preacher Man * Save Your Love

Can You Feel the Love (2007)

Disc 1: Can You Feel the Love * Singing the Blues * For the Good Times * Just Lovin' You (*Mary Duff*) * Hey Good Lookin' (*duet with Mary Duff*) * My Lovely Island Home * My Love for You * Walking After Midnight (*Majella O'Donnell*) * Have I Told You Lately That I Love You (*duet with Majella O'Donnell*) * Never Ending Song of Love * Hello Marylou * Mary from Dungloe

Disc 2: (Mio Carino) Maria * Are You Teasing Me (*duet with Mary Duff*) * Roses Are Red * Halfway to Paradise * Crush on You * The Power of Love * Tonight I've Held My Future * Until the Next Time * Heaven Around Galway Bay * Should I * Harbour Lights (*duet with Mary Duff*) * Wherever You Are * Tell Me You Love Me

Until the Next Time (2006)

Can You Feel the Love * My Love for You * Crush on You * (Mia Carino) Maria * I Forgot to Remember to Forget You * My Lovely Island Home * Tonight I've Held My Future * Don't Break My Heart * Beyond the Rainbow's End * Wherever You Are * Should I * Take the Hand of Love * You Gotta Feel Love * Love Me Or Leave Me * Until the Next Time

From Daniel With Love (2006)

Roses Are Red * I Love You Because * You Raise Me Up * Wind beneath My Wings * Save Your Love for Me * Flowers on a Sunday * Secret Love (*duet with Mary Duff*) * Burning Bridges * Tell Me You Love Me * Help Me Make It through the Night * For the Good Times * Love Me Tender * Talk Back Trembling Lips * I Can't Help It (If I'm Still in Love With You) * The Way That You Are * Honey * Moonlight and Roses * Stand Up for Love * Spanish Eyes * Wonderful Tonight

Early Memories (2006)

Disc 1: Bed of Roses * Forever You'll Be Mine * Excuse Me (I Think I've Got a Heartache) * Halo of Gold * The Streets of Baltimore * Geisha Girl * Life to Go * That's a Sad Affair * Bringing Mary Home * Crying My Heart Out Over You * My Old Pal * Our House Is a Home * Your Old Love Letter * 21 Years * Highway 40 Blues * I Wouldn't Change You If I Could

Disc 2: Home Sweet Home * The Banks of My Own Lovely Lee * Home Is Where the Heart Is * Dublin in the Rare Auld Times * The Green Hills of Sligo * Green Glens of Antrim * Blue Hills of Breffni * The Latchyco * Hometown on the Foyle * These Are My Mountains * My Donegal Shore * The Mountains of Mourne * I'll Take You Home Again Kathleen * Forty Shades of Green * Galway Bay * An Exile's Dream

Teenage Dreams (2005)

All My Loving * Calendar Girl * But I Do * Good Luck Charm * Heartbeat * Dream Lover * Poetry in Motion * My Special Angel * Be My Guest * Let's Twist Again * Ole Man Trouble * Only Sixteen * And Then I Kissed Her * Da Doo Ron Ron * You're Sixteen * With a Little Help from My Friends * Walk On By * Little Arrows * Words * Rhythm of the Rain

Songs of Faith (2005)

Softly and Tenderly * Sweet Victory * Here I Am Lord * Make Me a Channel of Your Peace * Put Your Hand in the Hand * Nearer My God to Thee * I Saw the Light * You Raise Me Up * Sweet Queen of Peace * Wind beneath My Wings * Footsteps * I Watch the Sunrise * My Forever Friend * He's Got the Whole World in His Hands (*Mary Duff*) * Let There Be Peace * Medley: Open Up the Pearly Gates/We Shall Not Be Moved * Lady of Knock * One Day At a Time * Panis Angelicus * Battle Hymn of the Republic

Shades of Green (2005)

Together Again * Sing Me an Old Song * My Happiness (*duet with Mary Duff*) * Coat of Many Colours * Tennessee Waltz * Medley: When Irish Eyes Are Smiling/ Green Glens of Antrim/Homes of Donegal/Boys from the County Armagh * Then the World Will Know * I Will Think of You * You're My Best Friend (*duet with Mary Duff*) * Wooden Heart * Medley: Daydream Believer/Come on Over to My Place/ Sweet Caroline/Show Me the Way to Amarillo * Medley: I Wonder Where You Are Tonight/The Little Things/Bed of Roses * Walk Right Back (*duet with Mary Duff*) * How Great Thou Art

Welcome to My World: 20 Classics from the Jim Reeves Songbook (2004)

Welcome to My World * Anna Marie * I Love You Because * When Two Worlds Collide * Am I Losing You? * Adios Amigo * How Can I Write on Paper * I Won't Forget You * Guilty * There's a Heartache Following Me * He'll Have to Go * It Hurts So Much * Moonlight and Roses * Blueside of Lonesome * This World Is Not My Home * Rosa Rio * Distant Drums * Four Walls * Don't Let Me Cross Over * Is It Really Over? * I Missed Me * Not Until the Next Time * You're the Only Good Thing

The Jukebox Years (2004)

Hello Mary Lou * Oh Boy * Do You Wanna Dance * All Shook Up * Three Steps to Heaven * When * Girl of My Best Friend * Come on Over to My Place * When You Walk in the Room * Daydream Believer * Sweet Caroline * Wonderful Tonight * Walk Right Back * Beautiful Sunday * Ob-La-Di, Ob-La-Da * Amarillo * Knock Three Times * I'm a Believer * Let's Dance * That'll Be the Day * Living Next Door to Alice

At the End of the Day (2003)

Sweet Queen of Peace * You Raise Me Up * Only the Shadow of Your Love * Sweet Heart of Jesus * Holy God We Praise Thy Name * Going Home * Hail Glorious Saint Patrick * Lady of Knock * When Darkness Falls * Queen of the May * God Be with You until We Meet Again * Let It Be * In Bread We Bring You * Surely the Presence of the Lord * May God's Blessings Surround You Each Day * At the End of the Day

Daniel in Blue Jeans (2003)

Singing the Blues * Teenager in Love * Never Be Anyone Else but You * Love Me Tender * Halfway to Paradise * Blueberry Hill * Bye Bye Love * It Doesn't Matter Any More * Travellin' Light * Fool Such as I * Roses Are Red * Save the Last Dance for Me * Donna * Send Me the Pillow That You Dream On * Wooden Heart * Young Love * Twelfth of Never * Honey * Green Green Grass of Home * Sealed With a Kiss

Yesterday's Memories (2002)

Sing Me an Old Fashioned Song * The Way That You Are * Yesterday's Memories * Help Me Make It through the Night * Tennessee Waltz * Coat of Many Colours * My Dreams Just Came True * Walk through This World with Me * When Two Worlds Collide * Blackboard of My Heart * Then the World Will Know * Tonight Will Never Happen Again * Even if It's Only for a Minute * I Can't Help It (If I'm Still in Love with You)

The Daniel O'Donnell Show (2002)

Stand Beside Me * Home to Donegal * Medley: You're the First Thing I Think of/I Don't Care/Back in My Baby's Arms Again * Waltz Across Texas * The Old Dungarvan Oak * Medley: Act Naturally/Excuse Me (I Think I've Got a Heartache)/Forever and Forever (I Love You) * I Heard the Bluebird Sing (*duet with Mary Duff*) * Vaya Con Dios (*duet with Mary Duff*) * Belfast * You're the Reason * I Can't See Me Without You * An Irish Lullaby * Galway Bay * My Shoes Keep Walking Back to You * Love Sick Blues (*Mary Duff*) * Our House Is a Home * Among the Wicklow Hills * My Irish Molly (*Mary Duff*) * Hello Darlin' * Only This Moment Is Mine * Green Green Grass of Home * Medley: When You Walk in the Room/Ob-La-Di, Ob-La-Da/Blueberry Hill/Let's Dance * Somewhere Between (*duet with Mary Duff*) * Top of the

World (*duet with Mary Duff*) * Roads of Kildare * I Just Want to Dance with You * The Rivers of Babylon * How Great Thou Art

The Irish Album (2002; re-released 2009)
Disc 1: Pretty Little Girl from Omagh * The Isle of Inishfree * Sing an Old Irish Song * Forty Shades of Green * Three Leaf Shamrock * Dublin in the Rare Oul Times * Blue Hills of Breffni * Green Glens of Antrim * The Old Dungarvan Oak * My Donegal Shore * Home Is Where the Heart Is * The Mountains of Mourne * Far Far from Home * Danny Boy * Any Tipperary Town * Irish Eyes * Our House Is a Home * Galway Bay * Come Back Paddy Reilly to Ballyjamesduff * I'll Take You Home Again Kathleen
Disc 2: An Exile's Dream * Heaven Around Galway Bay * Hometown on the Foyle * Lovely Rose of Clare * Roads of Kildare * Cutting the Corn in Cresslough * An Irish Lullaby * Dear Old Galway Town * The Banks of My Own Lovely Lee * Pat Murphy's Meadow * Destination Donegal * Lough Melvin's Rocky Shore * Mary from Dungloe * The Green Hills of Sligo * The Rose of Mooncoin * Your Friendly Irish Way * Limerick You're a Lady * These Are My Mountains * Home to Donegal * Belfast

Live, Laugh, Love (2001)
Live, Laugh, Love * Somewhere under the Sun * Green Green Grass of Home * On the Other Hand * Waltz Across Texas * Among the Wicklow Hills * Only This Moment Is Mine * All I Want Is You * Don't Say Love * One More Time * I Can't See Me Without You * Rosa Rio * I Will Think of You * Thank You for Loving Me * Roads of Kildare * Belfast

Faith and Inspiration (2000; re-released 2002)
Softly and Tenderly * Here I Am Lord * Morning Has Broken * Marriage of a Lifetime * Be Not Afraid * Light a Candle * Annie's Song * Nearer My God to Thee * Abide with Me * The Wind beneath My Wings * I Watch the Sunrise * Make Me a Channel of Your Peace * Let There Be Peace * The Rose * Battle Hymn of the Republic * Panis Angelicus

Greatest Hits (1999; re-released 2002)
Disc 1: I Just Want to Dance with You * Whatever Happened to Old Fashioned Love * Make the World Go Away * I Need You * The Magic Is There * Secret Love (*duet with Mary Duff*) * Four in the Morning * My Donegal Shore * Take Good Care of Her * The Way Dreams Are * Danny Boy * When Hope Dawns at Sunrise * Home to Donegal
Disc 2: Footsteps * Save the Last Dance for Me * My Shoes Keep Walking Back to You * Uno Mas * Stand Beside Me * There Goes My Everything * Timeless (*duet with Mary Duff*) * Singing the Blues * Beyond the Sunset * The Love in Your Eyes * Give a Little Love * The Gift * How Great Thou Art

Love Songs (1998; re-released 2002)
The Magic Is There * Then You Can Tell Me Goodbye * For the Good Times * Halfway to Paradise * The Way Dreams Are * Let Me Be the One * Spanish Eyes * Sealed with a Kiss * Hello Darlin' * Smooth Sailin' * Somewhere * Lay Down beside Me * Love Me Tender * Give a Little Love

The Magic Is There (single, 1998)
The Magic Is There * Thoughts of You * Twelfth of Never

I Believe (1997; re-released 2002)
Everything Is Beautiful * I Believe * Any Dream Will Do * I Can See Clearly Now * I Have a Dream * The Greatest Love * A Little Peace * The Way Old Friends Do * Rivers of Babylon * What a Wonderful World * A Song for the World * Even on Days When It Rained * Beyond the Great Divide * Our Special Absent Friends * Love, Hope and Faith * Desiderata

The Love Songs EP (1997)
Save the Last Dance for Me * I Can't Stop Loving You * You're the Only Good Thing (That's Happened to Me) * Limerick You're a Lady

Songs of Inspiration (1996; re-released 2002)
This World Is Not My Home * Footsteps * When I Had You * One Day at a Time * Amazing Grace * Why Me Lord? * You'll Never Walk Alone * You Needed Me * I Saw

the Light * It Is No Secret * What a Friend We Have in Jesus * The Family Bible * The Children Band * Yes I Really Love You * He Took Your Place * In the Garden * My Forever Friend * How Great Thou Art * Standing Room Only * The Old Rugged Cross

The Irish Collection (1996)
Pretty Little Girl from Omagh * The Isle of Innisfree * Sing an Old Irish Song * Forty Shades of Green * Three Leaf Shamrock * Dublin in the Rare Auld Times * Blue Hills of Breffni * Green Glens of Antrim * The Old Dungarvan Oak * My Donegal Shore * Home Is Where the Heart Is * The Mountains of Mourne * Far Far from Home * Danny Boy * Any Tipperary Town * Irish Eyes * Our House Is a Home * Galway Bay * Come Back Paddy Reilly to Ballyjamesduff * I'll Take You Home Again Kathleen

Timeless (1996) Daniel O'Donnell & Mary Duff
Timeless * We Believe in Happy Endings * I Won't Take Less Than Your Love * Whispering Hope * Have You Ever Been Lonely * I Heard the Bluebird Sing * Eileen McManus * Secret Love * Vaya Con Dios * Walk Right Back * Just Someone I Used to Know * Jeannie's Afraid of the Dark * Somewhere Between * Will the Circle Be Unbroken

The Classic Collection (1995; re-released 2002)
World of Our Own * Love Me * The Minute You're Gone * My Forever Friend * Follow Your Dream * The Old House * A Little Piece of Heaven * The Old Dungarvan Oak * Walk Right Back * Distant Drums * Little Cabin Home on the Hill * Lover's Chain * The Little Things * Mary from Dungloe * Just Walking in the Rain * The Old Photograph * Moonlight and Roses * I'll Take You Home Again Kathleen

The Hits Collection (1995)
Disc 1: I Just Want to Dance with You * Rockin' Alone * My Irish Country Home
Disc 2: The Love in Your Eyes * Ramblin' Rose * The Old Photograph * The Little Things
Disc 3: Singing the Blues * Lovers Chain
Disc 4: Whatever Happened to Old Fashioned Love * Somewhere Between (*duet with Mary Duff*) * Medley: Together Again/I Can't Help It (If I'm Still in Love with

You)/Please Help Me I'm Falling

Disc 5: The Gift * Someday You'll Want Me to Want You

Christmas with Daniel (1994)

An Old Christmas Card * Snowflake * Pretty Paper * I Saw Mommy Kissing Santa Claus * White Christmas * Christmas Long Ago * When a Child Is Born * Santa Claus Is Coming to Town * Christmas in Innisfree * Silver Bells * Rockin' Around the Christmas Tree * C.H.R.I.S.T.M.A.S. * Christmas Story * Silent Night * The Gift (bonus track on CD only)

Especially for You (1994; re-released 2002)

Singing the Blues * Leaving Is Easy (When Loving Is Hard) * She Goes Walking Through My Mind * Happy Years * Broken Hearts Always Mend * Guilty * Travelling Light * Come Back Paddy Reilly to Ballyjamesduff * Whatever Happened to Old Fashioned Love * Sweet Forget Me Not * You're the First Thing I Think of * It Comes and Goes * Silver Threads Among the Gold * Someday You'll Want Me to Want You * Lover's Chain * Never Be Anyone Else but You

A Date with Daniel O'Donnell Live (1993; re-released 2002)

Medley: I Need You (Intro)/My Shoes Keep Walking Back to You * Pretty Little Girl from Omagh * The Love in Your Eyes * My Irish Country Home * My Donegal Shore * Follow Your Dream * Whatever Happened to Old Fashioned Love * I Just Want to Dance with You * Our House Is a Home * Medley: Rose of Tralee/Dublin in the Rare Auld Times/Galway Bay * Never Ending Song of Love * The Wedding Song * The Mountains of Mourne * The Little Things * Somewhere Between (*duet with Mary Duff*) * I Need You * Medley: It's a Long Way to Tipperary/Pack up Your Troubles/If You're Irish Come into the Parlour/The Blackthorn Stick (jig)/Kennedy's Fancy (jig) * Stand Beside Me (playoff) * How Great Thou Art

Follow Your Dream (1992; re-released 2002)

Follow Your Dream * Welcome Home * Not Until the Next Time * Cryin' Time * Back in My Baby's Arms Again * My Claim to Fame Is You * Sweet Memories * I Just Want to Dance with You * The Love in Your Eyes * You're the Reason * Belle of the Ball *

Galway Bay * Destination Donegal * How Great Thou Art

The Very Best of (1991; re-released 2002)
I Need You * Never Ending Song of Love * Don't Forget to Remember * A Country Boy Like Me * She's No Angel * Stand Beside Me Eileen * Pretty Little Girl from Omagh * Danny Boy * The Wedding Song * My Donegal Shore * Letter from the Postman's Bag * The Three Bells * Our House Is a Home * A Loved One's Goodbye * Home Is Where the Heart Is * The Old Rugged Cross * You Send Me Your Love * Take Good Care of Her * Standing Room Only

The Last Waltz (1990; re-released 2002)
Here I Am in Love Again * We Could * Last Waltz of the Evening * When Only the Sky Was Blue * Heaven with You * You Know I Still Love You * Talk Back Trembling Lips * The Shelter of Your Eyes * When We Get Together * Ring of Gold * A Fool Such as I * Memory Number One * Look Both Ways * Little Patch of Blue * Marianne

Don't Forget to Remember (1987; re-released 2002)
Don't Forget to Remember * I Don't Care * Old Loves Never Die * I Wonder Where You Are Tonight * Don't Be Angry * Roses Are Red * Before I'm Over You * Take Good Care of Her * Pretty Little Girl from Omagh * Green Willow * Don't Let Me Cross Over * The Good Old Days * Pat Murphy's Meadow * I Just Can't Make It on My Own

I Need You (1987; re-released 2002)
I Need You * Sing an Old Irish Song * From a Jack to a King * Lovely Rose of Clare * Stand Beside Me * Irish Eyes * Dear Old Galway Town * Three Leaf Shamrock * Veil of White Lace * Kickin' Each Other's Heart Around * Medals for Mothers * Wedding Bells * Snow Flake * Your Friendly Irish Way * Lough Melvin's Rocky Shore * I Love You Because

Two Sides of (1985; re-released 2002)
Green Glens of Antrim * Blue Hills of Breffni * Any Tipperary Town * The Latchyco * Hometown on the Foyle * These Are My Mountains * My Donegal Shore * Crying My